The Future of Transportation

William (Bill) C. McElroy
Copyright February 2023
Updated May 22, 2023
ISBN **9798379108052**

Preface:

The act of moving items or ourselves from point 'a' to 'b' is considered transporting via transportation and we all have a need to do it. We use various means for doing it, from walking to supersonic aircraft, and we all pay for the privilege with our earnings, tax dollars, and health.

This booklet is about what we are doing to the world around us, and what we can accomplish in making transportation 'fun', 'safe', and 'inexpensive', if encouraged to do so.

Table of Contents:

Chapter # 01 – Introduction to Transportation:

Transportation Deprived: Americans love their vehicles and tend to hate public transportation even though it is safer, faster in many instances, and less expensive for most travel. See "Public Transportation Facts" REF: http://www.Apta.com

(Public Domain Picture is from 2004 Federal Highway Administration's Manual on Uniform Traffic Control Devices)

This author believes that the Interstate Highway System was the worst way to go and that a light rail system should have been the transportation system of choice. Light rail can use non-polluting electric energy instead of highly polluting fossil fuels and was around before 1900.

Light rail can be computer controlled to allow robot vehicles to self-guide from and to destinations. Light rail can be much faster with speeds up to several hundred miles per hour. Light rail only needs two-foot wide concrete or asphalt tracks and not trillions of tons of material for multilane highways that have to be rebuilt every 10 to 40 years.

Light rail can be used for transport of very heavy commercial loads, and for passenger loads on the same tracks. Light rail can last from two to five times longer than fuel driven vehicles.

Light rail can be designed for underground or on overhead lines thus, allowing for more space for buildings. Light rail can be built to go from building to building, even 30 stories in the air.

Our nation, along with many others will in about 50 years come to a halt as our fossil fuel supplies dwindle to a trickle, and our

Interstate Highways fall apart due to lack of repair and replacement funding. We will be back to the horse and buggy, if we do not now start planning for and installing light rail or other environmentally and cost effective transportation systems.

See this author's manuals "Border Security Solved with High Speed Rail: Generating Jobs using Existing Solutions" and "High Speed Rail: What you Should Know!"

Section # 01 – The Automobile:

When I started driving the price of a gallon of gasoline was $0.17 and the average car got 18 Miles per Gallon (MPG). In 1966 when I finally purchased a new vehicle the  price was $2,150.00 and that was for a Pontiac LeMans with an 8-cylinder engine, it was a 'hot' ride. Insurance costs about $25 per month.

(Public Domain picture is from https://www.pexels.com/photo/close-up-photo-gasoline-fuel-pump-4744707)

Over the decades the cost of gasoline went up to $3.00 or more, the cost of a similar vehicle to $28,000, and insurance $140 per month. In between there were new and used vehicles every 8 to 14 years due to each wearing out, or just falling apart. I estimate that I have spent over $50,000 purchasing five new vehicles since 1964, another $10,000 in maintenance, some $15,000 in insurance, $6,000 for an accident, and $100,000 on gasoline and oil. I also had to wash and wax, replace tires and wiper blades, and pay for license plates, driver's licenses, toll fees, and taxes.

Could I have invested nearly quarter million dollars in something better, perhaps?

Add to this that yes it was sometimes fun driving and getting to see places that are not near public transportation, but then again, driving is not fun, it is tedious, dangerous, full of unexpected annoyances, as well as expensive.

Section # 02 – Trucking:

Trucking falls into three distinct avenues, the first being the pickup that is owned and mostly driven by farmers, construction workers, and those that want the pleasure of a vehicle for pulling a trailer or a boat.

These can cost from a few hundred used, to well over $50,000 in 2023 dollars. The cost of driving is high due to the insurance, licensing, fairly poor MPG, and cost of tires and other maintenance.

The second is the 'Box Truck' owners that may be individual or company owned and is generally used for local business hauling of products.

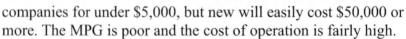

These can be purchased used from truck rental companies for under $5,000, but new will easily cost $50,000 or more. The MPG is poor and the cost of operation is fairly high.

Third is the 'Big Rigs' that may be called an 18-wheeler, semi-trailer, tractor-trailer, semi, or just truck and trailer. The engine and cab may be driver or corporate owned; the freight box is generally corporate owned.

The engine and cab will cost tens of thousands used, and well over $120,000 new. Cost of operation is very high in that MPG is super poor, and there are all sorts of government fees and restrictions.

Perishables and time sensitive items may be in jeopardy of spoiling or not arriving on time due to weather, no drivers

4

available, accidents, road closures, transportation cost, warehousing delays, loading delays, etc.

Section # 03 – Rail:

After leaving the USAFSS in 1964 I worked for American Brake Shoe & Foundry Co (ABEX) in Mahwah, New Jersey. Three of us designed and built the first 48-track route switching 'hump' yard controller.

A hump yard is where you back a multi-car freight train into the yard and release each freight car one at a time. The freight cars then free roll down an incline and are directed by automatic  switches to one of the individual tracks, in this instance one of the 48. After all cars are released you end up with not one, but 48 possible trains that are scheduled to go to 48 separate destinations.

(Picture is from https://www.bnsf.com/news-media/railtalk/service/hump-yards.html)

You then back in the next and subsequent trains and eventually all the new trains are full and hooked up to engines for their ride to their new destination. This can add several days to the trip for products that need to get from point 'a' to 'b', etc. Produce and other items that can spoil over time are jeopardized by this antiquated method of freight car sorting.

I worked as a drafting room manager for ComCenterCorp in Los Angeles for a period; we designed and produced a track signaling system for Amtrak that was used to track and partly control the trains as each moved up and down the coast. Hopefully the system helped in saving lives by preventing accidents.

My shop, AlScott Service Company, built a full room size model layout of the Ford Motor Company's People Mover system. Today, people movers are used in cities and at airports for moving people from area to area with comfort and speed.

I am a coauthor and publisher for the American Flyer Appraisal Guide, first edition, Stromroy Co.

I mention these experiences so that you, the reader, can get a feel for my passion of believing that we should have, and should now, go to light rail systems for the benefit of mankind worldwide.

Amtrak History and Ridership Cost

Amtrak is a passenger rail service that was born from the defunct and usually bankrupt rail lines of what are now either 'tourist' rail lines, or commercial freight rail lines.

Amtrak is owned by the USA taxpayers and has come under criticism by opponents of HSR as a waste of taxpayer dollars. The cost of operating the system is borne by the passengers, the limited mail and other freight, the snack bar, bar, and restaurant services that are on board. There are also travel guides and many 'interagency' and 'commercial' tie in agreements that produce some operating cash. But, that said the system does generally operate in the 'red' with only the Northeastern US corridor making reasonable profits.

So, why cannot the remainder of the system make a profit? The answer is that it is too slow for many and therefore, has limited ridership. These 'slow' lines and thousands of '5-MPH' type town road crossings; delays waiting for the commercial trains to open up track, and such put Amtrak into a situation where auto or aircraft transportation is just faster from point 'a' to point 'b'.

(Public Domain picture of California High-Speed Train)

A High-Speed Rail (HSR) system is being designed to eliminate these bottlenecks, and in fact many of the bottlenecks are being eliminated like the one near the Washington State / Oregon border. The National Gateway Project pushed by President Obama is eliminating throughout the eastern USA the low overpasses, the too small tunnels, and the bottlenecks that prevent double-deck rail cars from operating.

Rail has the advantage of taking the stress and the hazard content out of traveling; one sits back in comfortable seating, has tons of walking space, has restroom facilities and in some instances showers, has dining facilities, sleeping facilities if wanted, and has in many instances a bar, entertainment, and great sightseeing. The major disadvantages are the locations to airports and rental car agencies, and the limited number of long-haul trains.

REF: BorderTransportationSystem.com

More and more states, towns, and cities are turning to HSR for their transportation needs, as are dozens of nations around the world.

Rail is used for transport of goods and produce and the rule is that a freight train can be 17,000+ feet in length. (~3.1 miles). These long trains are bothersome to many people due to having long waits at crossings; lots of noise for an extended period, especially at night; and product delays due to short directional crossings (East vs. West bound passing areas). Some states and jurisdictions are now limiting the distance to 8,500 feet (~1.5 miles) in an effort to cut down on these complaints.

HSR and People / Freight movers operate differently in that the tracks are not tracks but channels that are raised above the ground. The propulsion is not a noisy engine but a quiet electric motor. The distance between units can be in inches and the number of individual units in a chain can be hundreds due to each doing exactly the same speed.

Section # 04 – Bus:

Short haul and touring buses need to have Commercially licensed drivers if the seating is over 15-seats, therefore many companies purchase 'Transit Vans' for their company needs.

(Picture is of a tour bus by https://www.davidtours.net/charters/fleet/tour-buses - this author use to provide Philadelphia tours to seniors using this excellent bus company)

These vans get good MPG, cost about $42,000 (2023 info), and drive and perform much like a car. There are individual state rules and regulations that you must follow if you are using one of these as a business opportunity.

These buses can be considered to be minibuses, transit buses, and shuttle buses.

Larger commercial buses can hold from 30 to 45 or more passengers and are used by touring agencies and professional transit companies. The government uses lower cost versions of these for school buses.

The majority of commercial passenger buses have elevated seating that is above the luggage compartment area. These are usually single deck buses and are the most popular. There are though double-decker buses that are used for touring in cities like Los Angeles and London. Where a city or town needs to carry many passengers they may decide to use an articulated (Banana, or Tandem) bus, especially on narrow streets that have tight corners.

Most of today's buses are powered by electric, gasoline, kerosene, or other fossil fuels. There are localities that are switching to Hydrogen, solar, or natural gas as a fuel.

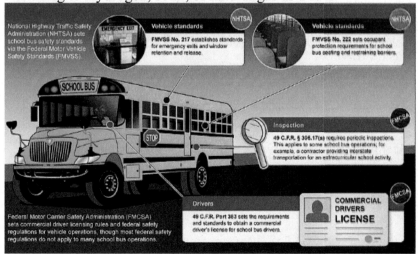

(Public Domain picture from the Federal Laws and Regulations and Department of Transportation Oversight Agencies for School Bus Safety)

School buses can cost from $90,000 to $290,000 and commercial buses can cost $550,000 or more. Drivers have to have a CDL (Commercial Driver's License) and be insured and perhaps bonded. Operating cost is high.

Section # 05 – Aircraft:

Aircraft come in various varieties that include military, commercial, freight, experimental, and personal. There are several engine classes from single engine prop to multi-engine jets.

All require specialized training and most require 'x' number of flying hours before one can even apply for the testing to pilot the next more complicated aircraft. The industry is heavily regulated and controlled and thus air travel is expensive. Safety and redundancy is a must.

(Public Domain picture of Baltic_Aviation_Academy_Airbus_B737_Full_Flight_Simulator_(FFS))

Air travel and airfreight shipping is highly affected by timing, weather, locations, type of aircraft, crew availability, crew knowledge, and cost. Air travel over international borders adds delays, an amount of anguish, and cost to the trips.

In the near future, 10 to 40 years from now we will be short on fossil fuels and therefore, most aviation fuels will be dedicated to our military and not to civilian use. If you do not believe this, then ask the military why they are developing battery and solar operated aircraft.

Section # 06 – Transportation Dangers:

Accident Specifications

The National Highway Traffic Safety Administration (NHTSA) reports that there are about 17,000 car accidents in the United States each day of the year, and that approximately 118 died in these accidents. This in turn has a cost in lives destroyed, but also in loss of productive employees, increased taxes, and increased insurance rates. It has helped the auto repair industry and the funeral home industry. If you add in the numbers of accidents in foreign nations, you may increase the negative effects of accidents by many fold.

MEDIA AVAILABILITY: FATAL COLLISION AND HAZMAT SPILL ON INTERSTATE 10 IN TUCSON

Thursday, February 16, **2023** - For Immediate Release - The Arizona Department ... at approximately 2:43 p.m. on Tuesday, February 14, **2023**, on eastbound Interstate 10 at milepost 272, in Tucson. When: Thursday, February 16, **2023**, at 1:30 p.m. Where: Arizona Department of Public Safety - ...

mhedblom - 02/16/2023 - 10:28am

As I write this, February 14, 2023 a truck carrying Nitric Acid overturned on I-10 near Tucson, Arizona. *(Picture)* The driver died and the spillage of the acid caused a 24-hour stoppage of all traffic on the highway, as well as having hundreds of citizens having to evacuate their homes and businesses due to the toxic and very poisonous fumes. The cost in lost productivity and emergency crews may be well into the hundreds of thousands. Those breathing the fumes may in the future develop lung and other serious health problems.

On February 15, 2023 the I-40 and several other northern highways closed down due to severe weather conditions, which may have resulted in lost productivity costing hundreds of thousands of dollars.

These are two of the thousands of incidents that happen each year around the world due to our insistence on NOT creating and using a safe transportation system; one of many, which we designed over a century ago before the automotive and oil industries took control of our lives.

Breakdowns

Vehicle breakdowns can be caused by debris on the roads, tires blowing, engines quitting, and transmissions failing. Each of these not only can cost money for reporting, towing, fixing, and loss of time and productivity, but also can be a danger to other traffic due to road blockage or pieces coming off the vehicle.

Driving Rules – Here and There

Each state and nation has its driving rules and if a licensed driver in one area decides to drive in another, there is a possibility that the lack of knowing the rules, signage, and laws can result in tragic and costly accidents.

For example, we have nations that drive on the left instead of the right as we do in the United States. We have nations that will not allow very young or very old citizens behind the wheel. We have signage that uses English, and others that use a foreign language. Each of these things may lead to driver confusion and possible trouble.

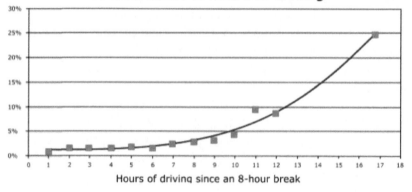

(Public Domain picture from http://www.fmcsa.dot.gov/rules-regulations/topics/hos/regulatory-impact-analysis.htm)

Night Driving

Nighttime driving is a challenge to all that drive in that one cannot see around corners or very far ahead of the vehicle being driven. This can easily lead to accidentally hitting another vehicle, a pedestrian, a biker, or an animal like a deer. Many times the driver will swerve to miss something or someone and therefore hit a tree, wall, or building. This too increases taxes, insurance rates, and decreases productivity.

Other Drivers

No matter what time of day you decide to drive you have to watch for Other Drivers that may be fatigued, putting on makeup, eating while driving, talking on a phone, sleeping while driving, thinking about work or home life problems, daydreaming, sightseeing, under the influence of drugs, or wiped out on alcohol.

Then there are those drivers that love to cut in and out of traffic, those that love to speed, those that feel they are better than you and can cut you off, those that are physically or mentally incapable of controlling a vehicle safely, and those that exhibit constant bullying and road rage. Each of these drivers is dangerous to your well-being and is costing good and safe drivers in increased taxes for law enforcement, and increased fees for insurance, both vehicle and medical.

Weather

Recently in 2023 the United State's southern tier had an ice storm that froze just about everything. Drivers

Vehicles pile up at the site of a fatal crash near Fredericksburg, Pennsylvania, Saturday, Feb. 13, 2016. The pileup left tractor-trailers, box trucks and cars tangled together across several lanes of traffic and into the snow-covered median.

were warned to NOT go out on the roads; many areas forbid drivers to go out on the roads.

So what did drivers do, they went out on the roads and found out that their high-priced four-wheel drive vehicles (and low priced two wheel drive as well) do not have four tires that can grip on ice, especially wet melting ice. The number of traffic accidents skyrocketed for a few days, and this cost lives and property, but also clogged hospital beds; put first responders in jeopardy, and cost taxpayers millions.

(2013 Picture is from https://weather.com/safety/winter/news/weather-fatalities-car-crashes-accidents-united-states)

 In states like Arizona there are wind and dust weather events that lead to many accidents as drivers fail to pull off the roads, turn off lights, and sit out the adverse conditions.

(Public Domain picture - https://en.wikipedia.org/wiki/File: Sandstorm_in_Al_Asad,_Iraq.jpg)

In several states there are tornados and naturally even if you are not driving, the vehicles get totally damaged from items being blown into each or the vehicle being lifted off the ground and dropped in a pile of broken glass and metal.

In most areas of the nation, world wide, there are rainstorms and floods that consume those vehicles and sometimes-foolish drivers in floodwater. It can be raining a hundred miles distant, but still be flooding the local creeks and highways. And again this adds up to more expense for motorist and governments, i.e. Taxpayers.

Add to this the cost of litigation between parties, and the cost of attorneys, adjusters, courts, and jail times for some 'accidents'.

Vehicle Design

Unsafe at any Speed by Ralph Nader was a book that changed the auto industry due to the industry's failure to design safety into their vehicles.

(Public Domain picture from ttps://commons.wikimedia.org/wiki/File:Ralph-Nader-1975.jpeg)

We have come a long way since the book was published, but we have a long way to go. There are too many accidents, injuries, and deaths on our roads and highways. We need to get back to enforcing the rules for building vehicles, especially passenger cars and trucks. There were rules on where headlights were allowed to be from the ground, both top and bottom. It seems that today's giant passenger trucks have headlights that shine directly in the passenger compartments of the average passenger car, which is a driving hazard.

We are equipping new vehicles with high intensity headlamps, and some, especially those that shine 'blue' that are blinding to oncoming drivers. Some manufacturers are using headlamps that only shine for a few feet above the ground, thus leaving items in the distance in pure darkness.

Many manufacturers in cost cutting moves have decided to go with minimum specifications on wheels, brakes, and bumpers. Body metal is thinner and crumbles or dents with very little force. Cushioned dashboards are back to being stiff and many contain hard plastics that can break and become dangerous weapons in a crash. Many dashboards contain silvered or mirror like trim that can reflect and blind a driver during sunlit days.

Most vehicles will still allow the driver to operate the vehicle without buckling up their seat belts. Rear view mirrors on many vehicles are too low and thus can obstruct a driver's forward and right-side views, as do the roof posts in both front and rear.

Section # 07 – Tourist Loop:

"At one time in our Nation's history we had the 'Tourist Loop' which included a highway loop that ran from National Park to National Park in Washington, Oregon, Idaho, Montana, Nevada, Wyoming, Arizona, and California. It connected Glacier, Yellowstone, the Grand Canyon, Yosemite, Olympic and others together and opened the West to tourism."

"Today we have millions of foreign tourist that are use to and love to travel by rail, and we should be considering reopening this 'tourist loop', with modern high speed and light rail systems that can produce billions of dollars per year for the USA and its business communities."

REF: BorderTransportationSystem.com

(Picture is from https://www.nps.gov/parkhistory/hisnps/NPSHistory/teddy.htm)

"Theodore Roosevelt, the noted conservation president, had an impact on the national park system extending well beyond his term in office. As chief executive from 1901 to 1909, he signed legislation establishing five national parks: Crater Lake, Oregon; Wind Cave, South Dakota; Sullys Hill, North Dakota (later designated a game preserve); Mesa Verde, Colorado; and Platt, Oklahoma (now part of Chickasaw National Recreation Area). Another Roosevelt enactment had a broader effect, however: the Antiquities Act of June 8, 1906. While not creating a single park itself, the Antiquities Act enabled Roosevelt and his successors to proclaim historic landmarks, historic or prehistoric structures, and other objects of historic or scientific interest in federal ownership as national monuments."

Chapter # 02 – Introduction to Fuels:

Fuel is a substance that can be converted to energy that can be used for propelling a vehicle; running equipment; or providing heat and light. This chapter is a summary of the various fuels we can and do use for propelling transportation devices, i.e. vehicles from point 'a' to 'b'.

(Pubic Domain picture is from Voice of America)

Section # 01 – Gasoline:

Gasoline and Oil Based Fuels:
Gasoline, jet fuels, and oils are being used at a rate that is not sustainable into the next decades and eventually will be depleted or so costly that only the super rich and the military will be able to afford each.

Most of the Oil today is in Russia, not Mexico or Canada, or in the USA or Middle East. The majority of oil producing nations needs the oil for THEIR people and their expanding economies.

Additionally, nations really do not want to be dependent on nations that have been or are adversaries, or that will be selling to competitors' worldwide.

President Obama and most people in America saw the writing on the walls and know our days of cheap and abundant oil are numbered. Railroads can run on electricity, which can be generated by coal, solar, wind, water, etc., and will be the ONLY inexpensive transportation by the year 2035. It will take much longer than that to connect most American Cities, even if we start

NOW, so America should STOP delaying what will be needed, embrace it, be part of it, and make money from it

The sun produces near infinite energy and thus should be the primary source of energy. It has been for thousands of years as the oil we use is basically stored sunlight energy. If you look to the past, about the 1960s, you will find that magazines like 'Popular Mechanics' were full of ideas on how to harness the sun's energy. Again, this is an opportunity for jobs and profits.

In recent years the advent of Horizontal Drilling and Fracking has increased the availability of Natural Gas and thus made it less expensive to bottle, transport, and use for home heating and cooking, manufacturing, and for public transportation. Many cities have converted their public buses and city maintenance vehicles to Natural Gas. It is reasonably clean burning, and if handled properly reasonably safe.

But, if it leaks, it can be very dangerous. This author lived in Philadelphia for a few years and witnessed first hand homes blown to smithereens; as well as had his home evacuated on a New Year's eve due to a gas leak. Using Natural Gas for passenger cars and light trucks may not be the safest use of the product.

Section # 02 – Geothermal:

This is a method of generating electricity using the heat of the earth.

(Picture is from the Middletown, California Geothermal Power Plant Visitor Center)

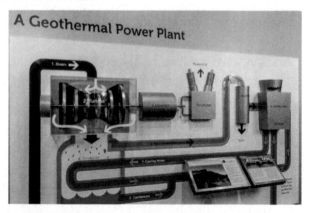

A Geothermal Power Plant

Middletown California

Middletown is about 80 miles north of San Francisco and just over the mountain from Calistoga. The geothermal field has grown considerably since I worked there some 40 years ago, and now covers 40 square miles and generates 1517 MW (Mega Watt) of power from its 18 power plants.

This is clean energy that is produced 24/7 in that it does not depend on wind or sunlight, it uses recycled sewage and waste water from the local towns and neighborhoods for its steam, and hot lava heated earth for converting the water to steam. The steam is used to turn turbines that generate electricity; when the steam cools back to water it is allowed to flow by gravity back to the hot mantle area where it once again becomes steam.

The wastewater used is currently being piped from towns as far as 30 or more miles distant. This is a win-win situation as it keeps the wastewater from polluting the rivers, lakes, and streams of the area while providing a constant source of water to the power plants.

The geothermal process is expensive to start, but low cost to keep going and maintain as there are few moving parts, and it generates nearly zero waste product, thus nearly zero pollution.

REF: https://geysers.com/Visitor-Center-and-Tours

Salton Sea in California

The Salton Sea in California is a 1905 mistake that happened when trying to contain the Colorado River decades ago; the low area got flooded with river water. When the leak was fixed it left a basin of water that over the decades collected dissolved minerals and salts from rains in the nearby hillsides. The only source of renewed water today is the infrequent rain and rain runoff from the nearby landscape.

At the southern edge of the Salton Sea Geothermal Field (SSGF) it was discovered that if you drill down you would hit the hot mantle and thus be able to boil water into usable steam for turning power generators. The Imperial Valley Geothermal Project has 14 plants and generates some 2250 MW of electric energy. As a byproduct of this area's energy production the plants also harvest battery-grade lithium hydroxide and carbonate for use in the EV auto industry.

Lithium Carbonate is valued at $12,000 per ton and the plants at this location are estimated to be able to recover 600,000 tons for a total value of $7.2 billion per year of operation in the 'Lithium Valley'

Additionally, the process can provide a good supply of manganese and zinc for other uses.

REF: https://newscenter.lbl.gov/2020/08/05/geothermal-brines-could-propel-californias-green-economy/

Section # 03 – Hydrogen:

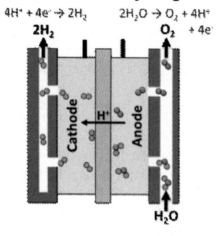

$4H^+ + 4e^- \rightarrow 2H_2$ $\quad$ $2H_2O \rightarrow O_2 + 4H^+$

$2H_2$ $\quad\quad\quad\quad$ $O_2 + 4e^-$

Cathode H^+ Anode

H_2O

There is a push to lower the cost of a Kilogram (US Gallon of Gasoline equivalent) of Green Hydrogen to $1.50 by the year 2025. Separation processes are done using electrolyzers or by using high-temperature electrolysis or by Methane Pyrolysis that uses high temperature to separate the Hydrogen; the CO_2 byproduct produced using this method is a solid and not a gas as results in other processes.

REF: https://www.science.org/content/article/hidden-hydrogen-earth-may-hold-vast-stores-renewable-carbon-free-fuel

There is different processing that is described by different color hydrogen as follows:

Hydrogen is a flammable gas that can be made from several substances or gasses that when ignited combines with Oxygen and forms a byproduct of water. If the process is a non-polluting energy source it is named 'Green Hydrogen' or (GH2 or GH2).

Green Hydrogen can be extracted from water, with water as a byproduct when burned. For each one molecule of Hydrogen extracted from water we get two molecules of Oxygen (O_2) that is the byproduct in the making of Green Hydrogen. To burn Hydrogen we need Oxygen as a catalyst.

Brown Hydrogen is from processing coal and the byproduct is CO_2, which is not wanted in the atmosphere.

Gray Hydrogen is from the processing of natural gas, and the byproduct is CO_2, which is not wanted in the atmosphere.

Blue Hydrogen is from Natural gas and the CO_2 byproduct is buried in underground storage.

Hydrogen is flammable and can be explosive and thus special care to prevent container damage or leakage is a must. There are several universities and companies that are experimenting with low cost means of extracting Hydrogen from water (H_2O) and storing it, using it, and making it feasible for use in passenger vehicles. Some government and corporate vehicles currently are using bottled Hydrogen for their transportation power.

REF: https://www.spglobal.com/marketintelligence/en/news-insights/latest-news-headlines/experts-explain-why-green-hydrogen-costs-have-fallen-and-will-keep-falling-63037203

Section # 04 – Nuclear:

Nuclear energy plants came to the US in the 1950s with the Indian Point nuclear plant built on the Hudson River just below

Peekskill and about 35 miles north of New York City. I was a young man on the day that it opened and was excited to visit and see this new energy source that was to revolutionize the world.

A decade later I got to work at the Mercury, Nevada Atomic Energy Testing site, sampling the results of atomic bomb explosions.

(Indian Point Nuclear Plant - https://www.nrdc.org/experts/kit-kennedy/indian-point-closing-clean-energy-here-stay)

The Indian Point facility permanently ceased power operations as of April 30, 2021, mostly due to some backroom shenanigans at the New York State governor's office.

REF: https://en.wikipedia.org/wiki/Indian_Point_Energy_Center

The cost of a nuclear power plant is high, but the 40 or more year depreciation is low and thus, the power-generating cost is reasonable.

Some people claim that the cooling water that is needed to keep the reactions under control is a hazard to boating and fishing and indeed, to some very small extent it is. Cooling water is obtained from wells or a nearby water source like the Hudson River, and then returned to the water source as warm to hot water. The Hudson River at Indian Point had a small dead zone that was off-limits to boaters and fishing. Some claimed that the plant was harming the local water supply, but that was unsubstantiated.

The intake of river or other natural water is screened to prevent fish and other items from entering the cooling towers, but microorganisms and fish eggs can, and in doing so are destroyed to the horror of many environmental groups.

The disposing of the spent fuel rods as a waste material is still in 2023 one item that is under contention and may never be settled.

Safety records over the last 60 or so years has shown that for the most part nuclear power is safe, but there have been three known plant failures due to natural events (Japan's Fukushima Daiichi), and a combination of mechanical and human failure (Three Mile Island & Russia's Chernobyl). Currently there are 440 nuclear reactors in operation supplying clean green energy in some 30 countries around the world. (2023 info)

Section # 05 – Solar:

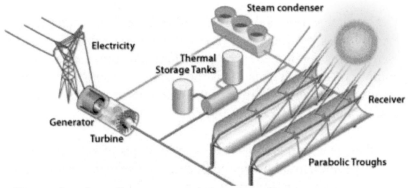

(Picture from https://www.energy.gov/eere/solar/linear-concentrator-system-concentrating-solar-thermal-power-basics)

The sun is shining and the air temperature is going up. In some parts of the world it gets so hot that you can cook an egg on the sidewalk or hood of a car. Solar heat or energy is a product of our sun that has been used as long as man has been on this planet. He or she has used it to start fires, warm dwellings, cook foods, and now to generate electricity using silicon chips that can convert sunlight to electricity.

REF: https://www.energy.gov/eere/solar/solar-photovoltaic-manufacturing-basics

The primary objection to solar cells is the lack of light during the nighttime hours and when there are too many overhead clouds; as no direct current (DC) is generated. Solar cells do NOT generate alternating current (AC) that is required for powering most items like your computer or television. There has to be a DC/AC converter in the power distribution line, and this adds to the overall cost.

The use of batteries for DC storage or other electrical backup systems helps to alleviate the lack of sunlight problems.

A secondary objection is that solar cells use energy for making each in the manufacturing process. This objection is easily overcome by using electricity produced by solar cells or other non-polluting Green Energy power.

The third objection is that there will come a time when the cells are no longer producing DC and will have to be discarded, and many worry about the leaching of chemicals into waste disposal dumps and groundwater. This too can be overcome by proper disposal methods and reuse of the materials. Replacement is usually in the 18 to 22 year old range of the panels.

Another objection is the use of land for acres of solar panels as used by commercial power companies in the massive solar farms. The companies have found ways around this objection by keeping the panels above ground and allowing sheep and other farm animals to graze under the panels.

Solar Panel sales and installation has become a major industry in many parts of the world, and the use of panels on home and business roofs is now commonplace. Although the panels will work in most areas, the best for home use are in areas or nations that are soaked in sunlight. We have in the US states like Texas,

Arizona, New Mexico, Florida, and California where sunlight prevails and the industry is spending billions on marketing solar.

Low cost solar panels and lighting can be used to cover sidewalks, bus stops, and for lighting yards, driveways, sidewalks, and out buildings. These are available as compact units with a cost of under $20 for the panel, a motion detector, and a light source.

Dirt and dust can reduce the power output of solar panels, but most areas get enough rain that the panels will remain clean.

Section # 06 – Methane Gas

Biogenic Carbon Cycle

CO_2

Hydroxyl Oxidation
Methane (CH_4) is converted into carbon dioxide (CO_2) after 12 years through hydroxyl oxidation

Cow manure and belches release carbon (C) as methane (CH_4)

Photosynthesis
Carbon dioxide (CO_2) is captured by plants as part of photosynthesis

CO_2 (Carbon Dioxide)

(Methane) CH_4

C (Carbon)
Carbon (C) is stored as carbohydrates in plants and consumed by ruminants

UC DAVIS
CLEAR Center

(Picture from https://clear.ucdavis.edu/explainers/why-methane-cattle-warms-climate-differently-co2-fossil-fuels)

People and animals produce manure and methane gas on a daily basis, and most of this is vented into the atmosphere. Farmers that raise large herds of cattle have found that if done properly they can trap this animal generated methane gas and use it for powering electrical generators for heating and lighting, and for powering tractors and other motor driven farm equipment.

REF: https://www.marketplace.org/2021/07/21/for-dairy-farmers-this-technology-turns-methane-from-cow-manure-into-cash/

Section # 07 – Waste Products:

Cities collect tons of waste each week and in many instances when the collection area is filled it is covered with dirt and grasses. Over time the waste rots and during the rotting process it generates methane. Using pipes inserted into the rotting waste one can collect the methane and pipe it to buildings for heating or to a generator for making electricity. To learn more on this, search for the Landfill Methane Outreach Program (LMOP).

REF: https://www.epa.gov/lmop

Trash burning can be highly dangerous due to the vast amount of dissimilar materials and the chemical makeup of each, but with proper exhaust fume treatments it can be done in relative safety. Many cities and towns burn the trash they pickup from home and businesses.

Some townships are turning trash into building blocks, and others are burying it so that it eventually becomes methane gas that can be retrieved and burned for generating heat and electricity.

(Public Domain picture - Garbage truck KAMAZ on the streets of Ulan-Ude)

Feces burning are being experimented with in several nations around the world, and in the US.

The Bureau of Environmental Services for Portland has a great system in place to make the most of its waste. The city's sewage is usually decomposed into methane gas, which is captured by their wastewater plants and turned into energy and electricity.

REF: https://eandt.theiet.org/content/articles/2017/11/the-power-of-poo-energy-from-excrement/

Wood from construction can contain all sorts of poisonous chemicals depending where it was used. Wood that is subject to high moisture areas may be impregnated with Chromated Copper Arsenate that acts like an insecticide and 'rot' prevention.

The burnt wood from construction may also contain any or all of the following:

Benzene, formaldehyde, acrolein, polycyclic aromatic hydrocarbons (PAHs), Chromated Copper Arsenate, creosote, ammonium copper quat, borate, arsenate, and hexavalent chromium.

Older wood from decades ago, perhaps an old barn building's wood, used chemicals like arsenic salts, copper sulfate, Pentachlorophenol, sodium dichromate.

Other chemicals that may be used due to the absorption rates of the particular wood are Ammoniacal copper arsenate (ACA) and ammoniacal copper zinc arsenate (ACZA), Acid copper chromate (ACC), and chromated zinc chloride

REF: https://www.buildinggreen.com/feature/pressure-treated-wood-how-bad-it-and-what-are-alternatives.

REF: https://www.epa.gov/burnwise/backyard-recreational-fires

Smoke and particulates are created whenever anything is burned. It does not matter if it is a piece of paper or a ton of coal, the exhaust smoke will contain particulates that can be harmful to life and objects. For example the particulates from burning coal can contain the following EPA reported substances.

The EPA Office of Air Quality Planning and Standards (OAQPS) sets National Ambient Air Quality Standards under the Clean Air Act for six principal pollutants, which are called "criteria" pollutants: sulfur dioxide, particulate matter, nitrogen oxides, ozone, lead, and carbon monoxide.

REF: https://www.gem.wiki/Particulates_and_coal

(Public Domain picture of Diesel smoke from a big truck. - U.S. Environmental Protection Agency (EPA))

Scrubbers are used to remove particulates from the exhaust of a furnace or other chemical reaction that if allowed to enter the air would pose a threat to humans, animals, live life, and items. The author has in the past designed small tabletop scrubbers for the integrated circuit industry. The design pulled contaminated air through a system of baffles where each was partly submerged in water. As the air flowed through  the container it had to enter the water and thus, it continued to flow, but the particulate was trapped in the water, to be disposed of at a later date.

Section # 08 – Water Related Fuels:

(Picture from https://www.energy.gov/eere/bioenergy/bioenergy-basics)

Biofuels are on the rise as technology and Research and Development (R&D) into the field increases. The idea is to raise biological substances like algae, corn (Shown), and grasses and use each to create fuels that can be somewhat non-polluting. Ethanol from corn is one of the primary biofuels that we currently use; it is an additive to gasoline.
REF:
https://www.energy.gov/sites/prod/files/edg/media/BiofuelsMyth VFact.pdf

Biofuels can be derived from many different plant sources, and from ocean water that may contain plastic particles, thus it may be an answer to eliminating some of the ocean contamination we are currently experiencing.

REF: https://www.theresearchpedia.com/research-articles/what-is-algae-fuel

(Picture from https://www.energy.gov/eere/water/articles/water-power-successes-2022-help-advance-clean-energy-goals)

Dams and power plants can generate a lot of electricity for use in residential, business, manufacturing, commutation, and transportation use. There are dams throughout the world that are working models of what is possible and what should not be. What many do not understand is that when you dam up a river or stream you may be producing a possible power source, recreational lake, or drinking water reservoir, but at the same time you are collecting silt and garbage, removing fish birthing grounds, and possibly creating a future disaster.

In addition, many of the western water sources are drying up and are near the point with there is not sufficient water for turning the turbines that generate the electricity.

> *"In an announcement on September 22, 2022 the U.S. Bureau of Reclamation (USBR) explained that updated hydrological models for the next five years "show continued elevated risk of Lake Powell and Lake Mead reaching critically-low elevations as a result of the historic drought and low-runoff conditions in the Colorado River Basin."*

REF: https://earthobservatory.nasa.gov/images/148861/lake-powell-reaches-new-low

Add to this the failure of several dams around the US and the world due to flooding and poor design or earth shifting movements. These failures are usually upstream from villages, roads, bridges, and parks that suffer severe and costly damages when the failure occurs.
REF: https://npdp.stanford.edu/dam_failures_us
REF: https://damsafety.org/Cost-of-Rehab

Hydrogen and Oxygen are two of the primary gasses that make up water (H2O), and these can be separated from each other to make Hydrogen (H) a flammable, and Oxygen (O) an oxidizer needed for combustion. This combination, if split, can become a very clean and inexpensive fuel source for use in transportation or generating electricity.

One negative is that most water is NOT pure, and therefore the contamination of viruses, minerals, particulates, and other items like our garbage and plastics may restrict the separation process.

Mineral Reclaims:

The use of ocean water for the

harvesting of Salt has been around for tens of generations and now we have found that oceans contain all sorts of minerals that can be harvested for use and profits. Mining Week website has a good listing of 40 minerals and how each is used and priced. Ocean mining is becoming a valuable asset to many nations as seawater contains hundreds of minerals, salts, vitamins, and other items we may consider necessities of life.

REF: https://seaagri.com/wp-content/uploads/2012/05/seawater.pdf

In addition, there are abundant fields of Kelp or Seaweed that cannot only be used as a food, but also as a fuel. And to retrieve the Hydrogen and Oxygen from seawater, new processes have been developed that can rival the freshwater processes.

REF: https://news.stanford.edu/2019/03/18/new-way-generate-hydrogen-fuel-seawater

In line water pipe power generation is also on the horizon in that many towns and cities, and eventually homes and businesses will be using the normal flow of water through the piping to turn generators that will generate electricity.

REF: https://www.power-technology.com/features/featurein-pipe-hydropower-urban-water-systems/

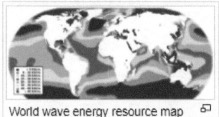

World wave energy resource map

Wave Energy is also a means of collecting motion that can be converted into usable electricity.

(Picture from

https://en.wikipedia.org/wiki/Wave_power)

REF: https://www.britannica.com/science/wave-power

Section # 09 – Wind:

A state like California tends to get winds twice a day due to the geography of the state and its nearness to the Pacific Ocean. Other states and nations may have similar geography that helps to create daily airflow or wind, and that wind can be used to turn turbines that can generate electricity. Wind Turbine speeds should be higher than 12 MPH and lower than 70MPH for proper operation.

In the past, windmills were used on farms, private residences, and towns to generate a means of mechanical power for machinery or for pumping water.

Today we have windmills that are much more complex in design and cost and can generate electricity that can power a single home or thousands of buildings. We have offshore anchored and offshore floating wind turbines, and we have on-shore individual or community turbines.

Generator cost is one element of the total cost of a commercial wind turbine. The total cost includes the construction of the tower mounting, the tower, the weather shielding, the gearbox, the DC/AC converter, and the three or more

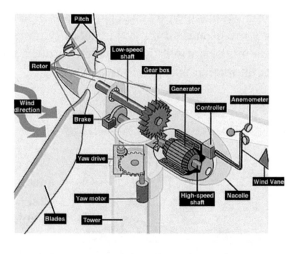

blades. For a home system the cost can run about $4 to $6,000 dollars; for a commercial system up to or more than $1 million.

(Public Domain picture -
http://www1.eere.energy.gov/webpolicies/#copyright)

Local fan blade production is normal for many of the large wind turbine fields for it is less expensive to make the blades locally than to transport each over hundreds of miles. Blades can be as long as 170 feet and thus would be restricted in many areas of travel.

Maintenance cost can be high due to the height of the turbines on the towers, but if maintained with regular inspections and lubricants, the turbines and generators should last 20 or more years.

"Whether you're a farmer, business, utility, or homeowner, wind energy as a renewable energy source outweighs the costs of wind turbines when viewed as a long-term investment from an environmental as well as an economic perspective."

"However, if you don't wish to finance your own wind turbine, leasing your land for a wind energy project or participating in a community wind sharing program are just two of the many options available today to homeowners, farmers, and small businesses."

REF: https://greencoast.org/wind-turbine-costs/

Section # 10 – Unknown:

Undiscovered sources of energy

Man is traveling out into space and also into the depths of our oceans and may in his or her travels discover that there is a power source that has been missed.

After all, we had no idea of Nuclear Power before we built the Indian Point Power Station in the 1950's, and we did not know that converting Silicon to Photovoltaic (PV) Wafers in the 1950's would revolutionize the power generation industry.

Add to this, we did not have the equipment for geothermal power generation until 1960, even though we used it since the Roman times for heating our bath water.

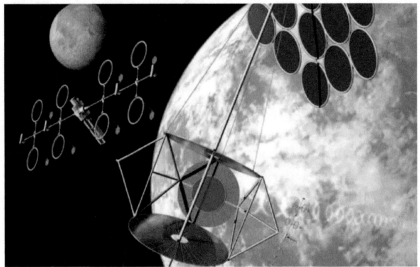

(Picture from https://www.bbc.com/future/article/20201126-the-solar-discs-that-could-beam-power-from-space)

The bbc.com website has interesting data on solar cells and other means of generating energy in space, including manufacturing on the moon, and several articles on how we may stop some of the Global Warming damage.

Chapter # 03 – Government Input into Travel:

Section # 01 – Environment:

(Picture from https://www.treehugger.com/cars-are-causing-air-pollution-we-breathe-new-study-finds-4856825)

Governments all over the planet are facing major transportation problems as more of their citizens desire to become mobile and are demanding faster and safer transportation. Roads, airlines, railroads, and shipping simply cannot accommodate the vast numbers of travelers without delays, accidents, and closings.

Manmade structures for travel are not just overloaded, but most are polluting the environment or destroying it due to the need for new right-of-ways. And as new right-of-ways are being constructed, the old ones are being abandoned and causing more pollution as each rots away.

The new right-of-ways are destroying nature in that trees, grasses, rivers, streams, and other natural structures are being ripped apart or covered over to be lost forever. Animals are being displaced from their birthing and feeding grounds, and are now seeking refuge in our towns and housing areas, which is unsafe for both they and us.

Protection of water and air supplies are a citizen as well as a governmental responsibility, and that means more regulations, more rules, and more taxation. It also means more discontent and hostilities as those seeking profits and other wealth face off against the environmentalist communities that seek content with nature.

Eventually, the convergence of these problems will be more than governments can handle or afford, and at that point we as a planet wide population are in trouble.

Section # 02 – Government:

Prime Minister Jean-Marc Ayrault introduced carbon taxes when he announced the new Climate Energy Contribution (CEC) on 21 September 2013.

(Public Domain picture from the US Dept of State)

Since then over 35 nations have implemented a carbon tax in an effort to slow Global Warming and harmful worldwide pollution.

"A carbon tax is a type of penalty that businesses must pay for excessive greenhouse gas emissions. The tax is usually levied per ton of greenhouse gas emissions emitted."

"Carbon taxes have been implemented in 35 countries to date. The United States has not enacted a carbon tax although a number of proposals for one have been submitted to the U.S. Congress."

"A carbon tax is paid by businesses and industries that produce carbon dioxide through their operations. The tax is designed to encourage such businesses to reduce their output of greenhouse gases and carbon dioxide, a colorless and odorless incombustible gas, into the atmosphere."

REF: https://www.investopedia.com/terms/c/carbon-dioxide-tax.asp

Trading Lots is a means for one company that has excessive CO2 emissions to pass the inspections by buying 'emissions trading system' (ETS) units from those companies that have little to no CO2 emissions. This trading system tends to average out the emissions and therefore cut the overall emissions.

REF: https://www.weforum.org/agenda/2022/07/carbon-tax-emissions-countries/

Government taxation of companies is a means of financing the infrastructures that are required for moving fuels and other items from the source to the final user. The Carbon Tax is used in an effort to get companies to change the ways they do business, and thus stop or limit the carbon pollution each emits.

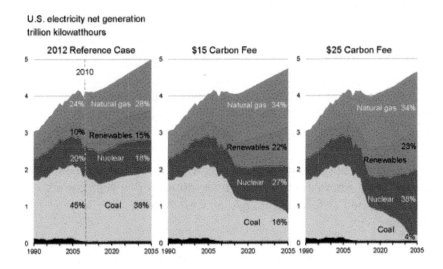

U.S. electricity net generation
trillion kilowatthours

Source: EIA, Annual Energy Outlook 2012

Carbon Taxes are somewhat regressive to the public, especially the less wealthy public as it taxes the fossil fuels that may be powering vehicles, heating homes and offices, and used for production of items. The more tax on the poor, the poorer the poor become. Thus, many states do not wish to pass Carbon Taxes.

> *"Despite being one of the world's biggest CO2 emitters, the US currently doesn't have a carbon tax at a national level (Feb 2023). But several states, including California, Oregon, Washington, Hawaii, Pennsylvania and Massachusetts, have introduced carbon-pricing schemes that cover emissions within their territory. President Biden has pledged to cut emissions by 50% by 2030 and achieve net-zero by 2050. But the concept of a carbon tax is regarded by his administration as politically risky and difficult to get passed in the US Congress."*

REF: https://www.weforum.org/agenda/2022/07/carbon-tax-emissions-countries/

Regulations are a must as without each the world would be hectic. People and companies want to profit from their talents, labor, inventions, and investments and some, not all, will try to profit at the expense of others in both money and safety. To protect people from those that will not voluntarily do so, a government will pass laws, rules, and regulations that can be enforced by fines, jail terms, seizures, or closings.

The transportation and its fuel source industries are highly regulated due to the International aspects of each, and the inherent dangers of each.

Note that a properly built HSR or People / Freight Mover system using Green Energy would eliminate thousands of regulations and associated enforcement cost, as well as reducing the need for a Carbon Tax.

A good site for reading about Government Regulations on Autonomous Vehicles and other transportation is at https://www2.deloitte.com/us/en/insights/focus/future-of-mobility/regulating-transportation-new-mobility-ecosystem.html

Section # 03 – Private Industry & Government:

Balking about cost is one of private industry's constants. No matter if it were free, some would somehow balk. So, there has to be, and there is an agreement between private industry and government that there are limits of what each can or will do to protect the public or solve problems, while collecting cash for their usages.

(Public Domain picture of Ohio train disaster that may have resulted from lack of proper regulations or the reversal of some regulations at the request of the railroad industry)

One of the largest contentions in 2023 is that there are private industries that deal in fossil fuels, i.e. coal, oil, natural gas, and wood. Fossil fuels pollute and cause Global Warming or at a minimum health problems for millions. Thus, the government wants to limit the production and use of these fuels, and the fuel industry wants to create more uses for their products.

The coal and oil industry feel that the environmentalists and their Green Energy products are replacing it. Some of the coal and oil companies are experimenting with new products that are more acceptable, but not aggressively enough to everyone's liking.

There are job gains and losses in the fuel industries in that those that have for decades been working the coalmines are being retired or retrained, and some governments are stopping those in the oil and oil-piping industries. In addition, those that sell the products like gasoline service stations are worried about losing customers as more opt for Electric Vehicles (EVs) and no longer need the oil based fuels.

It is to be noted that in the 2022/3 Infrastructure Bill there are millions for the purchase and installation of EV charging stations on Federal Highways throughout the US.

R&D costs money and developing new products can break the bank for some marginal companies. Research and Development is progressing in government laboratories, private industry, and in universities. Much research has already been done, and many of the proposals or inventions have been implemented, but there are political, financial, environmental, and emotional aspects to be overcome.

REF: https://www.bbc.com/future/article/20211103-can-renewables-replace-fossil-fuels

Section # 04 – Past Ideas on Power Generation:

Over the decades many inventors, writers, dreamers, and research people have come up with ingenious ideas on how to produce electricity for commercial use. Here are a few examples.

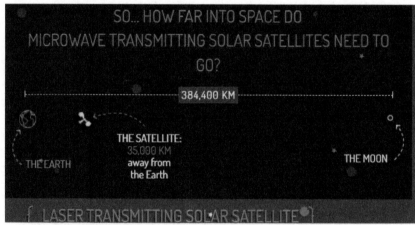

(Picture from https://www.energy.gov/articles/space-based-solar-power)

Microwaves from space have been considered for a few decades and the only thing stopping the implementation seems to be the will of the people to spend the hundreds of billions of dollars that would be needed to make it happen.

40

The idea is to install massive solar collectors in a stationary orbit where each can collect massive amounts of sunlight without blockage from clouds or other weather and atmospheric events. Then using either a cable that is anchored at ground level on one end and the solar collectors on the other, or using laser beams, or using microwaves the energy collected could be beamed to earth for distribution.

REF: https://www.energy.gov/articles/space-based-solar-power

Perpetual motion, as we know it is impossible due to friction between all items in both static and stationary states. But, if you get something cold enough, i.e. near absolute zero (-273.15 °C) the friction is nearly zero and there may be a chance to design a generator that will generate more energy that it consumes. There are laws of physics that say otherwise, but then again the 'earth is flat' as we once knew it to be.

Star Trek used an impulse drive that used a fusion reaction to generate highly energized plasma for some of its travels. It also used Dilithium Crystals for the warp drive matter-antimatter reactor. No such items, you may be right, but then again we do not know about everything that is out there in the blackness of space.

Section # 05 – Military Transportation Cost:

Our military is one of many that are protecting life around the world, and it has tens of thousands of vehicles that each requires fuel, maintenance, and storage.

(Public Domain picture - https://www.csis.org/analysis/us-military-spending-cost-wars)

41

Data from 2003 showed that our DoD (Department of Defense) spent some $7,000,000,000 transporting their people around the world. This does NOT include the cost of vehicles, aircraft, ships, mobile weapon systems, or the cost of sheltering each.

It is nearly impossible to actually determine the cost to the taxpayers of the individual transportation units due to the money being spread out among the various services and the inter-service departments, and due to purchasing schedules or needs at any specific time period. The following is an example:

REF: https://www.govconwire.com/articles/us-military-budget-2022-how-much-does-the-u-s-spend-on-defense/

What is known is that the military uses a lot of fuel and some of it cost as much as $400 per gallon as it needs to be transported to remote areas. During the Iraq and Afghanistan wars a single US army division could use 6,000 gallons of fuel per day

> *"In 2008 alone, approximately 68 million gallons of fuel were supplied per month to support U.S. military operations in Iraq and Afghanistan, and in the 2014 fiscal year, DOD consumed 87.4 million barrels of fuel ..."*

REF: https://www.army.mil/article/241758/driving_fuel_choices

The point is that if we convert to a lower and cleaner cost energy for our military transportation, the taxpayers can save not just billions but trillions of dollars; dollars that could be used for better transportation, medical research, and family security.

Section # 06 – National Debt and Highways:

In the last year (2022) I have traveled on I-8, I-10, I-17, I-19, I-40, and dozens of US-xx roads. NOT one was what one could consider safe or in decent condition as each were feeling the effects of weather, trucking, and aging. Each had miles of road being rebuilt, and most had unsafe bridges being torn down and replaced.

BUDGETARY RESOURCES — in millions of dollars

ACCOUNT	FY 2020 ACTUAL	FY 2020 CARES ACT	FY 2021 ENACTED	FY 2021 CRRSA	FY 2021 AMERICAN RESCUE PLAN	FY 2022 PRESIDENT'S BUDGET
FEDERAL AVIATION ADMINISTRATION	17,617.7	10,000.0	17,964.5	2,000.0	8,009.0	18,452.6
OPERATIONS (GF/TF)	10,630.0	0.0	11,001.5	0.0	0.0	11,434.1
FACILITIES & EQUIPMENT (TF)	3,045.0	0.0	3,015.0	0.0	0.0	3,410.0
RESEARCH, ENGINEERING & DEVELOPMENT (TF)	192.7	0.0	198.0	0.0	0.0	258.5
GRANTS-IN-AID FOR AIRPORTS (GF)	400.0	10,000.0	400.0	2,000.0	0.0	0.0
GRANTS-IN-AID FOR AIRPORTS (Oblim) (TF)	3,350.0	0.0	3,350.0	0.0	0.0	3,350.0
RELIEF FOR AIRPORTS (GF)	0.0	0.0	0.0	0.0	8,000.0	0.0
EMPLOYEE LEAVE FUND (GF)	0.0	0.0	0.0	0.0	9.0	0.0
FEDERAL HIGHWAY ADMINISTRATION	49,226.6	0.0	49,062.0	10,000.0	0.0	47,062.0
FEDERAL-AID HIGHWAYS (Oblim) (TF)	46,365.1	0.0	46,365.1	0.0	0.0	46,365.1

(Public Domain picture – This chart is in full on the following:

https://www.transportation.gov/sites/dot.gov/files/2021-05/Budget-Highlights2022_052721_FINAL.PDF)

We keep building new highways, of which each will need to be rebuilt in 20 to 30 years at a cost that will due to inflation be more than the original build cost.

In addition, in the last few weeks (Feb 2023) we have had to close I-8, I-10, I-17, I-19, I-29, I-70, I-75, I-90, and several other interstates due to accidents, weather, earthquakes, and rebuilding. Over a period of a year the cost to our state and federal governments runs into the tens of billions, and this is only scraping the surface as to what is really needed to 'fix' our broken infrastructure.

REF: https://usafacts.org/state-of-the-union/transportation-infrastructure/

We in conjunction with the use of the highways need to fuel the vehicles that use these highways, and that cost is the price of the fuel times ~377,000,000 gallons per day. (US data 2023)

REF: https://www.eia.gov/energyexplained/use-of-energy/transportation-in-depth.php

Times that by $0.184 the federal gasoline tax and we consumers are spending $69,368,000 per day just on the Federal Tax. Now add in the individual state taxes, and one can see where using a fuel like gasoline can and does represent a high price for the convenience of owning a car or pickup truck.

REF: https://igentax.com/gas-tax-state-2/

This cost is directly due to the inherent failures of using a highway system instead of more advanced public rail and People Mover systems. Not included in the cost of using fossil based fuels is the damage to the environment and to the health of all.

Section # 07 – What Other's are Doing

While the US sits back and does little to exploit the new transportation technologies the rest of the world are advancing and not only creating jobs, but also making money doing so. For example, we have China that has now captured the MagLev, and the High-Speed Rail markets in nations around the world. They are the number one supplier, followed by Japan, Germany, France, and South Korea.

China

China is selling MagLev to Saudi Arabia and Turkey. China's 20,000 Kilometers of high-speed rail makes it the number one manufacturer with a market share of over 60%. China is currently building a Shanghai to Hangzhou MagLev line that can reach speeds of 360-Km/h or 224 MPH.

Japan

Japan is selling their MagLev to the United States of America. Japan has been building HSR since 1960s and their Shinkansen trains rival the fastest in the world. Japan has a MagLev that operates as the Chuo Shinkansen line between Nagoya and Tokyo. This line has speeds that hit 505-km/h or 314 MPH.

Germany

Germany is selling their HSR systems to China, France, and Spain. Germany has the Transrapid MagLev that can transport you at 430 KM per hour. They are now the leader in MagLev technology. Germany's Transrapid MagLev uses synchronous motors that can propel their train at speeds upward of 450-km/h or 280 MPH.

France

France is selling their HSR systems to Italy, South Korea, and Turkey. France has the Alstrom Company, which is one of the world's largest supplies of HSR technology. France's TGV HSR can do 320-km/h or 200 MPH, as it glides along on 3,000 km or 1,864 miles of track.

South Korea

South Korea is selling their HSR to Turkey, the United Arab Emirates, and the United States. South Korea is working on building 4,000 KM of HSR by 2025. South Korea's KTX-II HSR reaches speeds of 300-km/h or 186 MPH, and they are or have built a line between Busan and Seoul.

Add to these are the following:

Canada

Canada with it Bombardier Zefiro HSR has been exported to Taiwan and other nations that wanted a 200-km/h or 124 MPH rail system.

Italy

Italy's Frecciarossa HSR that does 300-km/h 186 MPH on 1,000 km or 621 miles of track.

Spain

Spain's AVE HSR that can do 310-km/h or 193 MPH on its 2,000 km or 1,243 miles of track.

Russia

Russia that has the Sapsan HSR the does 250-km/h or 155 MPH on the Saint-Petersburg to Moscow line.

United States of America

The United States that has NO MagLev or HSR per se, and is bogged down in the development of the California HSR and the Amtrak proposed improvements.

Amtrak's Acela can in some short railways hit 200-km/h 124 MPH, but due to the rails, the crossing, and the other obstacles cannot maintain that type of speed over long distances. And yes, it has in short burst been able to hit 241-km/h or 150 MPH. It averages 125 MPH most of the time.

Robert Goddard in 1909 first proposed the MagLev and how to build it. The Germans (James Powell and Gordon Danby) in the 1960s built the first working unit at the Brookhaven National Laboratory.

In 1984 the British opened the first commercial MagLev, but then closed it in 1995.

In 2004 the Chinese started to operate their version of the MagLev and it has been in continuous operation.

Other HSR Developments are:

Africa – Egypt

There is a line being built by Japanese Company that will connect Cairo to Alexandria and allow for speeds of 250 km/h or 155 MPH. There has been talk of replacing the outdated Cairo to Aswan rail system and other shorter lines, as tourism is increasing and the need for safe and fast transport has developed. This talk has now resulted in a Chinese company signing a $9 billion contract for a 543 km HSR system.

Africa – Morocco

This African nation has a Casablanca and Tangier working line that travels the distance in two hours at 320-km/h or 200 MPH.

Africa - Kenya:

Kenya is in the process of building a line from Mombasa to Nairobi some 472 KM or 293 miles.

Africa – Nigeria
Nigeria's 400-km/h - 870 mile line is to go from Lagos to Kano.

Africa - South Africa
They are planning on a 800km – 500 mile HSR line from Durban to Johannesburg.

Greece
There is under construction a HSR from Athens to Thessaloniki and it is scheduled for completion in 2025. The estimated speed will be 250 km/h or 155 MPH. The line will eventually connect Thessaloniki to the Bulgarian and Turkish borders.

India
India has seven approved corridors for 320-km/h 200 MPH trains and is working on building each. The Japan International Cooperation Agency (JICA) is funding the construction of this.

Portugal
(See this author's books on Portugal and its tourism and rail systems.) Portugal is replacing track in many sections of the nation and is purchasing modified trains that can travel at over a hundred miles per hour on existing, yet older, track.

Turkey
This nation is expecting to increase tourism and is investing in its HSR systems. They have HSR from Ankara to Istanbul, Ankara–Sivas, and Ankara–Konya. The HSR travels at 250km/h or 155 MPR on most of the system.

United Kingdom
The HS(1) is the UK's first 300 km/h – 186 MPH train. They have plans for a HS(2) that will connect London to Birmingham, Manchester, and Leeds. The HS(1) connects the Channel Tunnel (Chunnel) to London, and is used by those wanting to travel to Europe and back. The UK has upgraded several of the older lines to carry passengers at 200 km/h or 125 MPH.

Section # 08 – People Movers

These are one to a few passenger cars or train that are on dedicated loop tracks and used mostly for airport gate to gate movement of passengers. The idea is to have a totally automated and driverless system that can be computer regulated as it travels for point a to point b at a reasonably fast clip. People Movers can be found in the following nations:

Argentina, Australia, Austria, Belgium, Brazil, Canada, China, Colombia, Costa Rica, Czech Republic, Denmark, Egypt, Estonia, Finland, France, Germany, Greece, Hong Kong, Hungary, India, Indonesia, Iran, Ireland, Israel, Italy, Japan, Jordan, Kenya, Kuwait, Lebanon, Malaysia, Mexico, Morocco, Netherlands, New Zealand, Norway, Oman, Pakistan, Panama, Peru, Philippines, Poland, Portugal, Qatar, Romania, Russia, Saudi Arabia, Singapore, South Africa, South Korea, Spain, Sri Lanka, Sweden, Switzerland, Taiwan, Thailand, Turkey, United Arab Emirates, United Kingdom, Uruguay, Venezuela, and Vietnam.

Although the People Mover was created as a hanging monorail almost a century ago, the United States instituted the first airport units at the Washington Dulles International Airport in 1962. (The author of this manual, via his company AlScott Service Company in Detroit, helped Ford Motor Company design and market their People Mover System via a working room size model of the system).

Currently China is the leader in building People Mover Systems and is building over a hundred (100+) as this book goes to print. This opportunity was an opportunity for the US to own the marketplace, but it failed and the jobs and profits are going to communist China.

Chapter # 04 – Future Trends in Transportation:

Transportation Opportunities:

The automobile and the pickup truck are the two primary means of transportation in the world. Yes, there are bicycles, motorcycles, trains, and aircraft available for getting from one place to another, and these are fine time-tested means of transport. Think about the cost and the pollution that is generated by fossil fueled vehicles. Not just the pollution for the burning of fossil fuels that produce a pound of carbon for every 25 miles driven, but also the cost and pollution from the millions of miles of road surface.

Concrete and asphalt are used in most areas to cover the dirt that was once used for 99% of our roads. These covering materials are costly and each does wear as millions of vehicles travel upon each. Additionally, there is the maintenance of line stripe painting, and applying salt and other materials to keep the roads dry and safe. All of this could have been prevented back in 1958 and 1963 by not selecting an Interstate Highway System, but a national rail system instead. Rail has many advantages over roads in that rail transport can be faster, safer, programmable, energy efficient, and longer lasting.

(Picture - High Five Interchange at the intersection of I-635 and U.S. Route 75 in Dallas, Texas, looking towards the southwest. - https://www.flickr.com/photos/fatguyinalittlecoat/2909850055/)

There has been massive objection to High-Speed Rail in the United States. Other nations have had HSR for decades and move millions of passengers per year at reasonable cost and great safety, using electric energy generated from the sun and wind.

Section # 01 – Autonomous Self-driving Cars:

We are on the way to owning or renting an autonomous self-driving car in that many of the latest models have backup cameras, no hands parking, lane change warning, lane following steering, automatic emergency braking, digital GPS mapping, GPS tracking, automatic speed controls, digital displays, all sorts of engine and other device warnings, and some have total hands-off driving.

There are many vehicles that are being tested and some do a very good job of getting from point 'a' to 'b' without hitting something or someone.

The Pros are that these vehicles can be designed to self-protect themselves and their passengers from accidents, and can allow a person to better relax without stressful blood-pressure increases from worrying about the others on the roadways.

The Cons are that the technology is not 100% and many of the features can fail; GPS can take you to places you did not expect to be; and lane tracking can be confused by poor lane markings, highway off-ramps, and bad weather.

Note that up until the car and the oil were available, we had one of the world's greatest railroad systems, and much of it was local and ran on electricity.

Section # 02 – High Speed Rail:

{Photo is from Alex Needham (own photography) on en.wikipedia and is Public Domain}

To many people High Speed Rail (HSR) is a 'dirty' word and a waste of taxpayer money, and to some extent history has played a part in this type of thinking. We had nationwide rail systems that were run by private industry, and many failed; the result was that we, the taxpayers, purchased the failed systems and created Amtrak, which to many is also a failed system. What many do not know, is that where Amtrak owns its right-of-way, the Northeast, the trains are making a profit, it is mainly where Amtrak does not own its right-of-way, but rents time on private freight tracks, and therefore is limited to slow speed, freight line schedules, and one-way only each day tracks, is where Amtrak is NOT making money.

Under several presidents and state governors, we are slowly updating tracks to eliminate delays, allow double height passenger cars, etc., so that we are obtaining 'semi-HSR', at about 120 to 140 mph. This is good, but it is NOT what we need, we need 220 to 300 mph rails and trains that run on electricity so that we can use Solar, Wind, and other commercially available electricity sources as a means of power, thus getting rid of fuel oils as the primary power. Magnetic Levitation would be the best as it can power single car trains with a minimum use of electricity, and there are no trucks (wheels) and rails to wear out, little to no vibration, speeds up to 500 mph, and track sections that can be manufactured in local factories.

Tourism:

(Picture from https://www.trade.gov/travel-tourism-industry)

The United States of America is one of the most visited destinations for worldwide tourism, and most of the foreign tourists spend a thousand or more dollars on airfare, rental cars, motels, restaurants, entry tickets, gifts, etc., when visiting. The vast majority of these 'foreign' tourists are from countries like Japan, China, and Europe that have had U.S.A. designed (originally) HSR systems, and therefore are familiar with 'riding the rails'. These tourists are on strict timetables and do NOT have the time to drive many hours or days between U.S.A. tour locations, this is especially true of the American Southwest, where our National Parks (NPS) are few and far between.

Our airlines cater to our Business communities, and NOT to our tourist industry, therefore places like Tucson, Benson, Willcox, Tombstone, Sierra Vista, and Douglas, Arizona are NOT fully or at all served by most direct flight airlines, or any airline. There is Amtrak rail and there was in the past rail services to these popular tourist locations, but in most instances no longer. A HSR People Mover System (HSRPMS) would open up these areas to tens of thousands of additional American and Foreign Tourist, thus bringing in millions of extra dollars to the local economies each year.

There are 'tourist' loops throughout the U.S.A., i.e., the Grand Circle Loop of the American Southwest that covers the Vermilion Cliffs National Monument, Bryce Canyon National Park, the Grand Canyon (North Rim), Zion National Park, and Lake Powell. Other nearby attractions include Grand Staircase-Escalante National Monument, Coral Pink Sand Dunes State Park, the privately owned Moqui Cave, and the largest animal sanctuary in the United States, Best Friends Animal Society.

Or, the great National Park to Park highway loop that was created decades ago and went to Rocky Mountain National Park, Yellowstone National Park, Glacier National Park, Mount Rainier National Park, Crater Lake National Park, Lassen Volcanic National Park, Yosemite National Park, General Grant National Park (now part of Kings 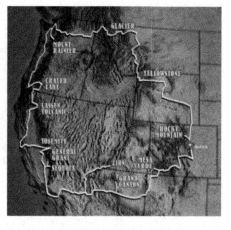 Canyon), Sequoia National Park, Zion National Park, Grand Canyon National Park, and Mesa Verde National Park.

(Picture from: https://www.nationalparkstraveler.org/2009/06/national-park-park-highway)

We are as a country building highways that will in less than 40 years become potholes and need to be totally renewed at a cost of tens of trillions of dollars. These highways will be near empty unless we convert a hundred million vehicles from fossil fuel to electric or other non-oil based fuels. We are already seeing fuel prices rise as tens of millions of foreigners gain wealth and use the limited amounts of oil that is available to the world. We are seeing airlines cut routes, increase numbers of seats, and increase prices to the point that many Americans can no longer afford to fly.

Tourism is a major, and may become our only, profitable industry and we are neglecting it by not making it easy to get to the places that people want to see. We should turn our attention from a business-to-business (B2B) HSR system to a Grand Circle, or National Park to Park System HSRPMS, that is powered by wind and solar along its full route.

Paying for this:

(Picture is Public Domain - AirTrain JFK seen from terminal 4.)

The beneficiaries of these HSRPMS systems will be private industry, the tourist industry, and our taxpayers via the state and national park systems, and Amtrak. There will be less traffic and thus wear on our roads (DOT savings), more people visiting our parks (NPS profits), less vehicle pollution (EPA savings), less forest damage (USDA savings), easier tracking of foreign nationals* (HS savings), and much more. Thus, each of these departments can and should contribute a portion of their budgets to the HSRPMS systems.

> *In Portugal we needed to show our passports everywhere and on every public transport we rode.*

Add to this the funds from private investors, the manufacturers of locomotives, solar and wind energy products, rolling stock passenger cars, and the local Chamber of Commerce, etc., we should be able to finance this without additional taxpayer monies. There will be a fee for the passage on the HSRPMS, and this can be as little as $0.05 per mile; which for the National Park to Park route of nearly 6,000 miles would generate $300.00 per passenger minimum, naturally there would be 'upgrades or adult pricing' that can bring this to $900 or more per rider. The $300 minimum is an affordable price for seniors and children as opposed to the nearly $2,700 that it would cost to rent a vehicle or drive one's own.

The Plus:

For a person to drive 6,000 miles around the National Park to Park System route would take some 100 hours or 12.5 days at 8 hours per day, therefore it will take 25 days to see all the parks, and additional hundreds for food, gasoline, insurances, and motels.

The same trip can be done in 12 days with people spending 5 to 8 hours per day seeing the parks, and sleeping or riding on the HSRPMS the remainder of the days. Sleeping berths can be available at $50 per night in addition to the normal coach seating prices, if a person does not want to spend overnight at a local motel or resort.

This HSRPMS system is the solution to many of our problems, it would put hundreds of thousands to work throughout the U.S.A., it would bring tens of billions of touring and tax dollars into the U.S.A., it would give Americans a better and more energy efficient way to see America, and it would cut down pollution, traffic accidents, insurance costs, and highway replacement and maintenance.

Talk to your Congress, and let's see what we can accomplish, especially realizing that this type of system can be used in most of the country to tie together our natural resources, our park systems, and our tourism industry.

Section # 03 – People Movers:

High Speed Rail People Mover System (HSRPMS)

People Movers ©
If you ever find yourself in the Denver Airport, you will probably find yourself taking a ride on the People Mover, a one car automatic robot controlled train that takes passengers from terminal to terminal.

(Public Domain picture, 2008 Denver International Airport Train)

This was developed in Detroit in the 1970s by companies like AlScott Service and Ford Motor Company. AlScott* did the working miniature model for Ford to test out the concept and sell the idea to others. The People Mover is now being used in many areas of the country for fast and efficient transport of people.

The People Mover was also called the 'Horizontal Elevator' since it acted like an elevator, a transport device that would move people and goods from location to location on demand, and not on a schedule as most buses and trains do.

Like an elevator, the People Mover can be used to move people and goods from building to building, and in between floors of any height. Thus, a city like New York that has skyscrapers can have People Movers at the first, second, third, or eightieth floors from building to building. We have the technology, and a system of People Movers from high-rise to high-rise in most cities would alleviate much of the surface transportation gridlock, while providing safe and efficient transportation of people and goods out of the weather and hustle and bustle of the city's streets. This would save energy, cut pollution, and allow vehicles to park miles away in secure parking garages that are also served by the People Mover networks.

The People Mover developed by Ford Motor Company (My shop was the initial designer of the fully working model that was used for the concept) is a single unit rail car that is self-propelled and programmable by the riders, who use the unit as a 'horizontal elevator'.

(Public Domain picture -
Detroit_People_Mover_crossing_Jefferson_Avenue,_July_2003)

Riding on a track system, or a cushion of air, it can reach speeds in excess of 200 MPH. Unlike bus, regular rail, and airline systems that have to work on set schedules, the People Mover is 'ON-Demand'.

Unlike most train systems that have set stations, the People Mover can have a station every 20 feet if that is what is needed, it does NOT stop at any of the stations along its route until called by a user to do so. Thus, if I want to get on in Detroit and off at the airport, I can, or I can take the People Mover to Atlanta if I wish. Unlike many of our public and private transportation systems that only run during the day, the People Mover would be available 24/7, and in most types of weather.

Unlike buses and aircraft, the People Mover can be designed to be nearly 100% safe, the concept and working systems have been

www.siemens.com/global/en.html

in use for over 30 years; the units are equipped with sensors that control speeds, avoid collisions, and self-diagnose and remove each if a potentially dangerous maintenance situation develops.

(Picture from https://www.mobility.siemens.com/global/en/portfolio/rail/rolling-stock/val-systems.html)

People Mover tracks can be 'prefabricated' in factories, and can be elevated to help prevent vandalism. Being elevated the tracks can be open to the air in 'U' shaped channels, thus very immune to weather, especially ice and snow that will fall through the track to the ground below.

The People Mover right of way can be the existing Interstate, Federal, and State highway system, and can also supplement or replace the passenger rail systems.

The 'track' design can contain solar and wind energy generators for the electric that will be used for much of the daytime power. The track can also be designed to carry commercial electric, natural gas, water, etc., to areas around the country, thus adding value and with the conduit rentals, help pay for the systems.

People Mover systems can also be brought into buildings, i.e. a building in an industrial park, and a single parking area can be built on the outskirts (multilevel) and the People Mover go from building to building within the park; and being an "On-Call' system, it can provide office to parking lot service on a moment's notice. This saves land, snow plowing in northern states, and development dollars as roads, street signs, traffic lights, etc., with the industrial park would be minimal.

REF: https://phys.org/news/2013-11-uk-town-deploy-driverless-pods.html

In cities like Philadelphia, the People Mover is a low cost alternative to building new highways to take up the ever-increasing volume of people traveling in and out of the city. Philadelphia, like most cities, have 'subways or elevated rail systems in place. This would replace the scheduled lines that if, missed can result in long waits, with an On-Call System that is much speedier and safer.

It is time to rethink our cities and the transport of people and goods.

* *AlScott was formed and owned by the owner of this website.*

Section # 04 – Autonomous Trucking:

Trucks the same as with the autonomous cars use technology that is not fully complete and therefore, a person has to be behind the wheel watching what the machinery is doing.

PROs are that there should be less accidents, lower insurance, and faster delivery of goods.

CONS are that you do not want to be the victim of an 80,000-pound vehicle crushing you to death out on the highway.

Section # 05 – Aircraft:

For distance travel and speed we depend on airline travel and the operational routes that have been authorized over the last several decades. The speed of many aircraft range from 350 to 550 miles per hour, but due to regulations, lack of personnel, weather, scheduling, maintenance, etc., the destination-to-destination speeds are significantly slower.

In today's world just to get to a seat on an aircraft can take up to three or more hours due to travel time, TSA, boarding, and more. Checking in, having your bags checked, being x-rayed and possibly searched by immigration and passport control, and waiting for the aircraft to be cleaned and serviced; along with loading and then the taxing to the runway and its waiting time all contribute to the demise of speed.

If you are traveling internationally, then you have further delays in the customs and immigration offices at the foreign terminals. You may be subjected to more baggage checks, more documentation checkpoints, and the possible need for Visas, Passports, Medical Vaccination Cards, and Global Entry Passes.

As discovered in the latter part of 2022 the weather can also play havoc on getting off the ground or landing at the chosen airport; cancellations and days of waiting time frustrated millions of flyers,  and the businesses that could not get their products to the marketplace. One airline alone was forced to cancel 3,000 flights on December 26, 2022.

(Picture from https://www.faa.gov/newsroom/faa-daily-air-traffic-report)

What many citizens do not know is that some airlines are taxpayer supplemented for flying routes that are totally non-profitable, and in many instances are total losses of revenue. The Federal government subsidizes these routes so that someone or some business can travel the route at your expense.

Taxpayers also subsidize the Air Traffic Control (ATC), the TSA (Transportation Safety Administration), the Immigration Customs and Border Protection (CBP), and the National Transportation Safety Board (NTSB). The airlines, which are private companies each benefit from the taxpayers via these agencies.

Add to this is the fact that aircraft are massive polluters of our atmosphere and are slowly harming the planet.

https://www.transportenvironment.org/challenges/planes/airplane-pollution/

Some of the pollution from highflying aircraft are nitrogen oxides (NOx), CO_2 carbon dioxide, soot particles, and sulfate particles.

I have been a passenger on aircraft from the 1950s to the current 2022 year, and have seen the change in the air over the decades. The air in the 1950s was clear and at 33,000 feet you could make out cars, houses, streams, roads, etc. At 33,000 feet on the most recent flight from Arizona to Portugal and back I could barely see the ground for most of the trip, the air was too thick with pollution, especially at the 30,000 to 35,000 foot level where most commercial jets fly.

Section # 06 – Pneumatic Tube Transport:

(Public Domain picture "The Pneumatic Dispatch" (pamphlet), American News Co. via Google Books)

Although the Hyperloop came into being in 2013, it is not a new invention as companies and others have been using pneumatic tube transport since before 1780. The idea is to use a vacuum to suck an object, and a pressure to push the object from its insertion point in a closed tube to its received point, and was used for sending mail and messages from room to room, or floor to floor in buildings. Many banks still use the system to send coils from the office area to the cashier areas. I believe that the CP.pt train system in Portugal uses pneumatic elevators for transporting passengers from one station level to another.

"In the 1960s, Lockheed and MIT with the United States Department of Commerce conducted feasibility studies on a Vactrain system powered by ambient atmospheric pressure and "gravitational pendulum assist" to connect cities on the country's East Coast.] They calculated that the run between Philadelphia and New York City would average 174 meters per second, that is 626 km/h (388 mph). "

REF: https://en.wikipedia.org/wiki/Pneumatic_tube

By using both gravity and large fans, one can design and build a system that allows a train or 'pod' to start at an above ground location, move downward by gravity at increasing speeds, then using momentum move upward to the exit point. This is a proposed first track between New York City and Washington D.C.

REF: https://www.businessinsider.com/history-hyperloop-pneumatic-tubes-as-transportation-2017-8#researchers-at-mit-designed-a-vacuum-tube-train-system-for-a-45-minute-trip-from-new-york-city-to-boston-in-the-early-1990s-like-musks-plan-the-design-called-for-a-magnetic-track-8

(Public Domain picture - Yucca Mountain nuclear waste repository)

This could not have been possible in the 1960s due to the technology and machinery lacking for digging long and deep earth tunnels. Today we have tunnel making machines that can not only dig long and deep, but also line the tunnel with reinforced concrete as it moves forward. Today's tunnel machines may be able to operate at 21,600 feet per day or 4 miles per day, and that would therefore only take 51 days for digging the tunnel from NYC to Washington, DC. (In ideal conditions)

An added advantage is that the depth of these tubes will or could protect millions of citizens in the event of a nuclear attack or an alien invasion. My recent book *'Underground Cities (A*

Traveler's Guide)' has instances that date back before Christ where people used underground tunnels for transport in an effort to escape capture, slavery, injury, or death.

Getting permission to build these tunnel trains is another thing.

Section # 07 – Hyperloops:
A New Hyperloop Test Track Is Being Built In Las Vegas

"Hyperloop Technologies announced on Monday that it will start building a test track at the Apex Industrial Park in the City of North Las Vegas, Nevada."

"If you've never heard of the Hyperloop before, it's basically superfast tube transportation system. Using tunnels that have all the air sucked out them, pods slip up and down the tubes at high speeds. The company hopes the pods will eventually be able to accelerate to over 1,100 kilometers (700 miles) per hour. The system boasts a particularly  *eco-friendly design, using only electricity from renewable sources."*

The idea was originally envisioned by SpaceX CEO Elon Musk (picture) in 2013. However, he allowed it to be taken up by entrepreneurs to be developed. Two separate companies have picked up the baton since then – Hyperloop Technologies and Hyperloop Transportation Technologies. This latest project is from the former, but confusingly, that's not the same company that is building the proposed track in California."

Read more on this exciting technology at:
http://www.iflscience.com/technology/hyperloop-technologies-begin-building-las-vegas-test-track-next-month

To see the currently proposed Hyperloop transportation routes in the US, see the https://www.inverse.com/article/30029-hyperloop-one-11-routes-across-the-united-states website. They show maps of several proposed routes with the time and energy savings that each will accomplish.

The differences between the Pneumatic Tube Transport and the Hyperloops is that the Pneumatic Tube Transport is mostly underground and requires very little purchase of surface lands, and the Hyperloops are above ground and will require purchase of right-of-ways, or be constructed on top of our existing highway systems.

There is also the difference in that Pneumatic Tubes depend on gravity for the majority of their power, thus nearly free power, and the Hyperloops depend on differential air pressure created by the use of large fan networks that may be aided by engines or MagLev.

Additionally, the Pneumatic Tube system is in the dark of a tunnel and may not be appealing to clients, whereas the Hyperloops are above ground and clients can view the landscapes.

The Pneumatic Tube has the advantage of doubling as a bomb shelter whereas the Hyperloops do not.

Section # 08 – MagLev:

(Public Domain picture - Transrapid series 09 vehicle at the Emsland Test Facility, northern Germany).

Magnetic Levitation roads and vehicles that can be driven on a normal street, alley, or road and then enter the MagLev track for 250 + MPH travel in safety and comfort from one city to another may be an answer. We designed these in the 1960s, and someday when governments get with it, we may actually have this futuristic means of transportation. There are foreign nations that already do have MagLev track and trains in operation.

The 500 MPH vehicle.
No, not High-speed trains, but something like it. I-10, I-40, I-17, I-25, I-80, I-90 are Interstate Highways with 'right-of-way' and large wide lanes and medium strips. Now, we have the 'magnetic levitation' technology, and have had it for decades; if we use the Interstate's free space we can build two lanes of MagLev. Solar cells and wind turbines every few miles can power these, and the idea is to NOT get rid of the automobile, but help it. You drive your vehicle onto a 'flat-bed truck' that is computer controlled and Mag Lev; this can then transport you safely at 500 MPH to your exit, where your vehicle can then again run on electric,

gasoline, hydrogen, or biofuels. The system prevents and is designed to not be prone to crashes or derailing from the track system. It can be instantly programmed to change routes if needed.

> *"This core feature is what's most exciting to Jesse Powell. "With MagLev, there is no driver. The vehicles have to move where the network sends them. That's basic physics. So now that we have computer algorithms for routing things very efficiently, we could change the scheduling of the entire network on the fly. It leads to a much more flexible transportation system in the future," he said."*

REF: https://www.energy.gov/articles/how-maglev-works

Japan Has this and it works

We allowed our technology to be taken over by Japan some 46 years ago, and today they have not only the world's first MagLev train, but are exporting the technology to the USA and the rest of the world.

We have a Washington, D.C., company that is now working with the Japanese to bring some of this technology back to the USA.

Section # 09 – Vactrain:

You may have never heard of the Vactrain, but it has been around since 1799 when George Medhurst of London conceived of and patented it as an atmospheric railway.

> *"In 1888, Michel Verne, son of Jules Verne, imagined a submarine pneumatic tube transport system that could propel a passenger capsule at speeds up to 1,800 km/h (1,100 mph) under the Atlantic Ocean (a transatlantic tunnel) in a short story called "An Express of the Future""*

> *"The Vactrain proper was invented by Robert H. Goddard as a freshman at Worcester Polytechnic Institute in the United States in 1904. Goddard subsequently refined the idea in a 1906 short story called "The High-Speed Bet" which was summarized and published in a Scientific American editorial in 1909 called "The Limit of Rapid Transit". Esther, his wife, was granted a US patent for the Vactrain in 1950, five years after his death"*

REF: https://en.wikipedia.org/wiki/Vactrain

Section # 10 – Personal Rapid Transit:

(Picture is of a PRT mockup at the Coach Museum in Lisbon, Portugal)

Personal Rapid Transit (PRT) is an innovative urban public transport system jointly developed by the design firm Pininfarina and Vectus Intelligent Transport. It is a lightweight, driverless vehicle, which can be deployed on networks of interconnected tracks. The following website has a write up with pictures.

REF: https://www.railway-technology.com/projects/personal-rapid-transit/

Section # 11 – Autonomous Aerial Vehicles (AAVs)

We may see the day we are the 'Jetsons' but I rather not as we have enough problems with things flying around as it is. People will be crashing into houses, poles, mountains, and others. Plus this will necessitate a new host of laws, licenses, and fees. The idea is nice to think about, but not practical and each will be costly to build and maintain. Plus, we will need a new traffic control system.

Section # 12 – Shipping & Cruises

Not to be overlooked is the vast amount of shipping of freight and the dozens of river and ocean cruise lines. Ships have for decades used wind, nuclear, and fossil fuels for their power sources. But this is now changing in that many are finding that it may be less expensive to make fuel on-board as they travel from place to place. Hydrogen is a great fuel if used properly and can be extracted cheaply from water. Up to now the process took lots of energy to do; the cost was high; and the size of the equipment is huge. But, if you have a giant ship, you can make room for the equipment, and you can use river or ocean water. Thus, it is possible for a ship to make its fuel as follows:

November 10, 2022

(Picture from the Viking website)

The Hydrogen powered Viking Neptune was built in the Fincantieri shipyard in Ancona, Italy. The Viking Neptune will spend its inaugural season sailing itineraries in the Mediterranean before embarking on the company's 138-day 2022/23 Viking World Cruise.

Please note that the ship was NOT built in the US, we gave up our shipbuilding and associated jobs decades ago. The last large commercial ship, a passenger liner to be completed in the United States was Moore-McCormack Lines' SS Argentina in 1958.

REF: https://www.travelmarketreport.com/articles/Viking-Takes-Delivery-of-First-Partially-Hydrogen-Powered-Cruise-Ship

Chapter # 05 – Jobs in Transportation:

The transportation industry can provide tens of thousands of good paying jobs to those with or without a college education.

Section # 01 – Construction:

(Picture from https://hsr.ca.gov/jobs - Shows just a few of the proud workers from the 9,000 jobs have been created building high-speed rail in the Central Valley in California.)

The following is from the BorderTransportationSystem book by this author; it is a listing of jobs that can be created just in this one high-speed rail project.

Jobs, Jobs, Jobs
One of the prime benefits to the *BorderTransportationSystem* is the fact that it will produce immediate jobs for hundreds of people, and then thousands of jobs for thousands of people, and eventually millions of jobs, on both sides of the U.S.A. / Mexican border. This can then be expanded to Central and South America.

Immediately, there will be a need for designers, drafters, engineers, managers, attorneys, accountants, bookkeepers, artists, marketers, and a host of support personnel. Then during the build stage there will be opportunities for truckers, heavy equipment operators, construction workers, planners, inspectors, testers, electricians, plumbers, metal workers, drywall and plaster contractors, roofers, flooring and tile installers, painters, welders, carpenters, etc.

During the build stages there will be a need to build the rolling stock, both freight and passenger rail cars, which will take designers, engineers, sheet metal workers, plumbers, electricians, fabric workers, window glass installers, iron workers, welders, carpenters, etc.

Once up and running there will be a need for cooks and servers, utility personnel, cleaning crews, inspectors, customer service representatives, ticket agents, parking lot attendants, medical personnel, presenters, maintenance personnel, loading / unloading personnel, etc.

Naturally, there will be all the existing Border Patrol and immigration jobs as well as national security personnel.

After the *BorderTransportationSystem* is completed there will be industrial parks, tourist opportunities, fisheries, cemeteries, waste disposal plants, water purification plants, and dozens of other specialty establishments created that would not normally exist without the *BorderTransportationSystem*.

Section # 02 – Generating Energy:

The United States and the world will need increasingly more amounts of good reliable clean green energy if each is to continue to develop and serve its citizens. That means more power sources, more distribution lines, more storage capability, more checks and balances, more accounting, and more revenue cost and generation. Each of these needs will produce good paying jobs and a better tax base for other needs.

Section # 03 – Service and Maintenance:

There was a day when an owner of a vehicle could change parts, tune engines, and do other adjustments using simple hand tools. Today's vehicles require highly trained technicians using advanced tools and microprocessor-controlled analyzers.

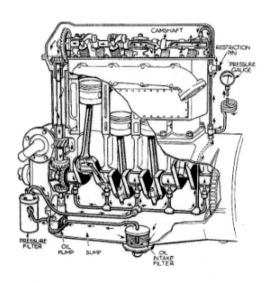

In the future the vehicles will self-diagnose, self-tune, and be so modular that even untrained owners will be able to switch out components within minutes. What will be needed are the assemblers and technicians at the factory level that will build, troubleshoot, and refurbish these modules.

(Public Domain picture of an overhead cam engine with forced oil lubrication (Autocar Handbook, 13th ed, 1935).jpg)

Section # 04 – Jobs That Will Disappear:

When the automobile is totally computer controlled it will no longer need a steering wheel, brake pedal, steering column, windshield wiper control system, light control system, and other controls that once needed manual manipulation by the driver.

The on-board computer will automatically control each of these functions without human intervention. This therefore, means that several industries will disappear over the decades long transition period from driver control to full computer control.

The change from fossil fuels to non-fossil fuels will also create unemployment in the fossil fuel industry, but not as dramatic as one would think. Fossil material such as natural gas and oil are used for many other items than fueling a vehicle. We will still be using asphalt in some areas; plastics for much of our 'stuff', and natural gas for heating and cooking.

The coal industry will suffer, but only due to the use of Natural Gas and other fossil and non-fossil fuel products.

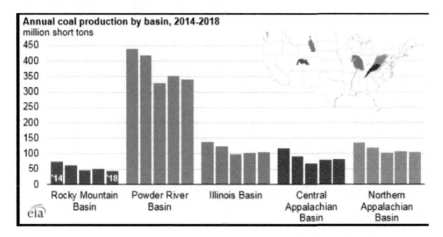

(Public Domain picture U.S. annual coal production by basin, 2014-2018 (31930259427).png)

And the complaint that we are putting miners out of work due to environmental hazards is totally bogus. The coal industry changed from digging tunnels in mountains to bulldozing the entire mountains to the ground, thus using a few dozer operators to replace dozens of miners. Massive environmental problems have developed due to this practice.

We will still need fueling stations in many of the rural areas where farming equipment is being used, and in areas that are too shaded for adequate solar generation of electricity, i.e. south side of mountainous valleys.

Currently there is a move from having filling stations supplying gasoline to supplying batteries or battery recharge stations. When the entire electrical system is up and running and all vehicles are attached to it, there will be no need for any filling stations.

Section # 05 – Where Do We Get the Money?

Rider-ship on Amtrak has been going up and up for the past three decades and it will continue to do so, thus when the bottlenecks to speed  are removed, the system will draw millions of commuters from new towns and cities that are hundreds of miles distant from the jobs in existing cities.

There are millions of Baby Boomers that are becoming Senior Citizens and who will have the time and money to travel the USA, they too will add to the overall revenue stream.

Europe, the Middle East, North Africa, and other lands that were once stable and good tourist spots are now in a flux and will be for a decade or two. These people want to vacation in a safe zone, and the USA has the safe zones and the world-class vacation spots. This will increase rider-ship and bring outside money into the USA by the basketful.

Parcel post services like UPS, USPS, and FEDEX will be using the system for moving packages, they already have started to do this, but when train speeds rivals airline speeds and the cost is less, they will use the Amtrak systems.

If the system is done right, and Amtrak owns many of its Alternative Fuel Power sources, it can produce enough extra fuel that it can sell to the power grids and make a profit doing so. The high wire supports that are above the trains can easily support tens of thousands of miles of solar cells and each station can be wind powered using Wind Turbines as well as solar and biofuels.

Right-of-Way Costing
Someone asked me about the money required to purchasing the Right-of-Way for the High-Speed rail systems throughout the US, and I had to think about it for a millisecond.

Amtrak already owns its rails in many sections of the Northeastern US, and it can join with the Commercial Carriers to add rails next to theirs as they already have much of the right-of-ways.

Additionally, in the mid to west routes the land is reasonably inexpensive; just ask the Oil Companies who are buying up properties for their pipelines.

We have millions of miles of old worn out highways, thousands of now closed rail lines that are spurs, and tens of thousands of miles of Interstate highways with both side and center areas that are for future expansion, but that can be used.

Additionally, the current rail lines, highways, and waterways can be double decked and the new upper decks can be used for 300+ MPH trains, or for MagLev 500 MPH trains.

If we do not invest in ourselves:
High-speed Rail production means that we will need ergonomic design engineers that can come up with new and more efficient rail cars that can meet the needs of various types of travelers from the new borne to aging seniors.

High-speed Rail production means newly designed and engineered locomotives that use a combination of diesel, natural gas, solar, regenerative braking, and electric energy as the trains travel from region to region and the fuel supply and cost varies.

 High-speed Rail production means newly designed and engineered signaling and control systems that can sense track and power supply conditions and take immediate action if necessary. Example: In the event of a flooded track or an earthquake, or a vehicle or person on the tracks, etc. the system will shut down. Japan already is ahead of us on the earthquake sensing controller designs.

(Public Domain picture - German railway signals (Hp system)

What does it mean if we do NOT create High-speed rail?
USA JOBS... That is right, we are allowing tens of thousands of USA jobs to NOT be created by NOT supporting HSR and the billions of dollars of potential exports to places like Russia, Europe, the Americas', Australia, Africa, Mexico, and Canada.

REF: BorderTransportationSystem.com

Section # 06 – Economic Competitiveness:

"Moving the U.S. workforce and its products in a quick and productive manner increases economic competitiveness. Traffic congestion wastes time, money, and petroleum. Freight rail can ease congestion by moving freight off highways, while commuter trains will give commuters a non-highway option. Rail can be an attractive choice, particularly for Intermodal trips over 500 miles. For the 100 to 600 mile trip between city centers, passenger rail travel, without lost time at airports for security checks and queuing in gate areas, can provide a competitive option that offers business travelers minimum loss of productive time when traveling between city centers. Moreover, as stated earlier, significant investment in a high-performing rail network will have far-reaching job-creation and economic benefits that improves America's manufacturing base."

REF:
https://dotcms.fra.dot.gov/sites/fra.dot.gov/files/fra_net/1336/NR
P_Sept2010_WEB.pdf

Section # 07 – Millions left Behind:

One has to realize that the use of the automobile is not available for everyone. People under age, people over age, the handicapped, the mentally challenged, or to sick to drive, and those that are non-citizens may not be allowed to drive, rent a car, or get a driver's license.

This is discrimination of a sort and is detrimental to not just the individual's life, but to society in general. We have one of the worse public transportation systems of any nation in the world, and we are also being left behind by many nations that are developing HSR, People Movers, and Personal Transport units.

Nations like Portugal treasure and respect their children, pregnant women, aging seniors, and their handicapped. You get to a crosswalk, everyone stops for you and some even get out to help you cross. You get on a bus or train and there are seats assigned to you, and if someone not in your situation is there, they get up and offer you the seat.

See author's books on Portugal for travel, food, and entertainment information.

Chapter # 06 – Future Predictions:

This chapter contains the author's predictions of where future transportation systems will be. The predictions are based on the types of transport needed, the cost of transport, the speed of transport, the availability of power distribution, and the environmental impact of transportation devices.

Section # 01 – The Availability of Fuel:

(Picture is from https://www.offshore-technology.com/features/the-future-of-oil-and-gas-predictions)

As more and more people have the desire to travel, the amount of fuel necessary will diminish to the point where fuel is priced out of the hands of billions of citizens. We are heading there, and our oil companies are not only seeking further and more difficult to drill and process fields, but are in 2023 pouring money into alternative means of energy production.

I predict that we will essentially run out of fossil based fuels (Oil, gasoline, jet fuel, kerosene, diesel, natural gas) by the year 2050. We will by then be nearly 100% dependent on green energy, mostly wind and solar that is converted to electricity.

The question is can we get the energy we need from other sources that are not dependent on wind or sunlight. For example, geothermal is becoming more possible as drilling techniques are getting better and we can drill deeper, thus closer to the hot magma that surrounds the earth at the mantle.

Capturing sunlight using satellites that are in fixed orbits over a town or city can be converted to microwave energy, beamed down to earth, and converted to electrical energy. Sounds far fetched, but we have considered this since the 1960s and the technology will soon advance to the point we can do it.

Converting water (H_2O) to Hydrogen and Oxygen is already being done. The cost is at present high, but as technology

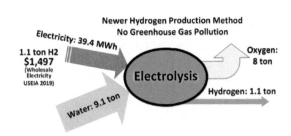

advances the cost will drop and you may someday be purchasing a low cost conversion unit for home or office use. The waste product of burning Hydrogen in an Oxygen environment is water (H_2O).

> *(Picture is in pubic domain, from https://commons.wikimedia.org/wiki/File:Hydrogen_production_via_Elec trolysis.png)*

Nuclear is safe, but the disposal of the spent material is not, so once we find a safe way of disposing or using the spent fuel rods, we will or should advance our technology and build more plants.

We are also experimenting with Nuclear Fusion, the opposite of Nuclear Fission, both of which can produce megawatts of electricity and do so reasonably cleanly.

> *"Both fission and fusion are nuclear reactions that produce energy, but the processes are very different. Fission is the splitting of a heavy, unstable nucleus into two lighter nuclei, and fusion is the process where two light nuclei combine together releasing vast amounts of energy."*
>
> *REF: Duke Energy.*

For a detailed write up on Nuclear reactions the following has a good amount of information (Feb 2023) - Habib Ur Rehman Sun, February 12, 2023 at 1:14 PM MST·8 min read

REF: https://www.yahoo.com/now/10-most-advanced-countries-nuclear-201431166.html

Section # 02 – The Cost per Mile of Transport:

In 2023 the cost of a gallon of gasoline is around $3.00 per gallon on average, and vehicles that obtain 25 MPG will use $12.00 worth of fuel for every 100 miles driven. In the years to come the price of fossil fuels will continue to rise as it did from $0.17 per gallon in 1960 to $3.00 per gallon in 2023, an increase of ~18 times in 60 years. Note that many vehicles got 14 to 18 MPG in the 1960s and therefore the cost per mile was about a penny.

Vehicle travel seems like the way to go, you buy a car, keep it, fill it, and eventually sell it and that is the total cost, or is it…

Actually, the USA taxpayer is paying for the Real Estate to purchase the right-of-way, the engineering for the construction, the construction, the monitoring by the 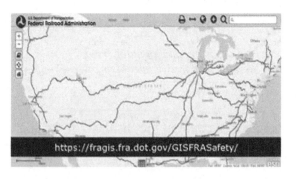 DOT (Department of Transportation), the monitoring by the police and fire departments, the maintenance of the signs, lines, guard rails, pavement, drains, islands, overpasses, underpasses, and the bridges, and most of this has to be rebuilt or repaved every 10 to 20 years.

(Picture from https://railroads.dot.gov/maps-and-data/maps-geographic-information-system/maps-geographic-information-system)

There is also the cost of limiting the air pollution caused by burning gasoline and other fossil fuels; this air pollution generates CO2, dirt, acids, and chemicals harmful to the environment, the water supplies, and the health of the citizens breathing the dirty air; these cost are 'hidden' but add tens of billions to the Bill the taxpayers have to pay each year. There are also the added cost of the anti-pollution equipment on the vehicles, and the cost of yearly inspections and possible maintenance. Industries like farms, seafood, fishing, etc., are suffering from the airborne and waterborne pollutants associated with vehicle and gasoline use.

There will be costs in building HSR, but most will be eliminated and will save the users much. In addition HSR will be electric and can use clean alternative non-polluting energy.

Here is an idea on how to pay for our transportation systems in the US. For each employee that drives to and from work each day, the company should have to pay $1.00 into a National Transportation Fund... This 'surcharge' (you know those things they put on us when gasoline was $4.00 per gallon and then never removed when it fell to $3.35.) can be used to fund the highways, airlines, and rails of the USA. That $1 would bring in about $160,000,000 per day every day of the year.

After all, we taxpayers have been subsidizing the rails, airlines, and roads for these company's profits for over 230 years, it is time that they pay us back. We also can and should ...

$$$$$$

Take 1% from the military subsidy, 1% from the Homeland Security subsidy, 1% from the Farm Subsidy, 1% from the Oil company's Subsidies, 1% from the Coal Company Subsidies, 1% from the Cotton Growers Subsidies, 1% from the State Department's budget, 1% from the Department of Energy's budget, 1% from the Airline Subsidies, 1% from the Highway Funding, 1% from the salaries of the top 5% of Americans, 1% from the Corporations that will each benefit from the system, and you have a ton of money to spend on building something that can be expanded from Alaska to the tip of Chile and benefit nearly a billion people and their job base.

Section # 03 – The Requirements for Speed:

As food production increases to keep up with demand, not just in the US, but also worldwide, we will need faster delivery of the food that is picked and processed. Currently up to 40% of the food production is wasted due to long travel times and the lack of transportation when needed.

Throughout the world we have a tourist trade that is a major financial element for towns, cities, states, and nations. Traveling from one tourist location to another takes time, and time is money. So if you can speed up their transport from 'a' to 'b' you may be now able to add 'c' as a destination. This author recently in 2022 traveled to Portugal, and their rail system, although not as fast as it is possible, did allow for seeing several places that ordinarily would not have been possible, except by wasted hours of car or bus travel.

To make speed possible we will have to rethink our transportation by doing several things.

The first is to dedicate trucking lanes on all major highways. This will allow the large trucks to travel at faster speeds and not cause complications that frequently develop when meeting slower vehicles, i.e. accidents.

(Public Domain picture by Lisa M. Macias, U.S. Air Force)

Second is to totally remove trucking from some or all long distance travel by converting or adding a lane to the existing Interstate Highway that has been converted to a Freight Mover High Speed Rail System (FMHSRS).

We could consider airlines, but building an airport near each and every food plant, field, or warehouse would not be practical. Only high value foods like Lobster can take advantage of an expensive five-hour coast-to-coast flight.

Section # 04 – The Environmental Impacts:

We are learning more about our environment, both inside our homes and offices, and on the outside in nature. We are beginning to understand how burning anything can cause all sorts of

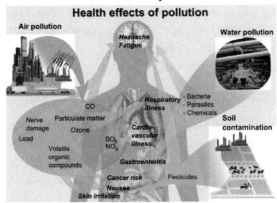

negative results that include major health risk. We are also learning that we have and do generate billions of tons of waste that leaches chemicals into the ground and groundwater, and that this waste contains harmful bacteria and viruses that cannot just sicken us, but kill or mutilate us.

(Picture - Häggström, Mikael (2014). "Medical gallery of Mikael Häggström 2014". WikiJournal of Medicine 1 (2). DOI:10.15347/wjm/2014.008. ISSN 2002-4436. Public Domain.)

We are currently seeing our western reservoirs drying up, and our glaciers disappearing due to both natural and man-made causes. Many communities get their water from slowly melting glaciers and these glaciers get recharged each year from snowfalls that top off the ice, and melt into it. When the glaciers are gone, there will be very little to hold snow and rain in the higher mountainous elevations, and thus in the heat of summer and fall there will be next to no water flow to the population below.

This lack of rain, snow, and glacier melt is also causing the reservoirs to dry up to the point that not only are those that depend on the water in trouble, but also that those that depend on the electricity power from these reservoirs will be in trouble. This is why in some southwestern locations like Tucson, Arizona there is a push by the electric companies to go Green, with wind and solar as a replacement for the electric power from the Hoover Dam.

I predict that as we learn, we will be passing more rules and laws, and there will be more congressional debates, but in the end the people will prevail as they learn about the health problems and associated costs that currently prevail.

Section # 05 – New Housing Projects:

Building roads costs money and housing developers do NOT like to spend money that they do not have to spend. In some areas of the world the housing developer will upon completion of the overall project turn the project over to the local township and thus things like sewage and water piping, sidewalks and streets, etc. become a taxpayer burden. This has in many districts caused the local township to pass road construction laws that increase the likelihood that the development will NOT need the roads replaced every few years.

(Picture is of the Rua de Santa Catarina in Porto, Portugal. The trolley tracks and the vehicle access stops at this point, and only pedestrian foot traffic is allowed for the next several blocks.)

As a means of eliminating this expensive cost, the future developers will eliminate roads within housing projects, and either only provide an exterior parking lot area with sidewalks to the housing, or provide an exterior parking area with a single track people mover type public transport. Not only will this save money in not building a complex network of streets, but also it opens up land for building more housing, and utilities can be under the homes.

This can also reduce the prices of building homes in that garages would not be needed, therefore the extra $50 to $100 square foot of space can be used for other needs, or totally eliminated for valued savings.

Section # 06 – Neighborhood Power Generation:

As the cost of transformers, wind turbines, and solar panels come down; more of each will be used on private property and by homeowner associations (HOA) for generating local electricity. Housing developers may include these faculties in their developments and thus have a future income source for decades.

Note that the last place one should install a solar panel is on a building's roof, as that means that when the roof needs repair or replacement the panels have to be removed, stored, and reinstalled. A better place for solar panels is over the top of sidewalks where each can not only generate energy, but also provide protection to people from the elements, i.e. rain, snow, ice, birds, sunlight, UV rays, etc.

Section # 07 – Crime Rates:

The crime rate in the world will go down when we all convert to public transportation due to there being no need for vehicles and the secondary market of 'stolen vehicle parts'. Yes, there may be some stolen bus and train parts, but since these will be part of a worldwide system that monitors the parts by the minute, the idea of stealing a bus or train part will be nearly unthinkable.

Additionally, with today's vehicles a criminal can detour off a main highway, rob a store, and be back on the highway within a minute. Having a 24/7 monitored public transportation system that can be stopped and locked tight within seconds of a robbery should discourage such activities.

85

Example:

When I owned AlScott Service Company in Detroit there were many robberies where a team of thieves would drive up on the sidewalk with a sliding door cargo van, open the door, kick in the window of a store (Usually one selling high-end electronics) and then rush in, load up what they could, and be back out on the street in less than 60 seconds. Storekeepers and insurance companies lost millions and many went out of businesses or like myself ended up with insurance premiums that made it impossible to continue in business.

By using only public transport the crime rates will go down, the effect would be that insurance rates would also go down, thus saving businesses and homeowners tens of billions each year.

Section # 08 – Lower Cost:

By using public transport as needed, the cost of ownership of a vehicle can be eliminated, no vehicle, no vehicle maintenance, insurance, car washing, trade in, lost value each year, no gasoline taxes and no state license taxes, no registration fees, no  garage, and no driveways needed. Think about it, how much do you spend on these items in total each year, hundreds or thousands of dollars.

(Public Domain picture of Flexity outlook 4403 heading south, 2014 08 31 - Toronto, Canada)

In addition, no worry about running out of fuel, no worrying about having the correct change at the toll booth, no worry about cleaning snow and ice off the windows, no worry about frozen door locks, no worry about your children playing with the shifter, no worrying about hail or shopping cart damage, and on and on.

Yes, ownership currently provides you with mobility security, and that is great, but if we actually had decent and safe high-speed public transport to our front doors, would that not be a much better choice?

Section # 09 – City Traffic Elimination:

Any of the track systems can be used for moving people and goods from building to building, and therefore instead of traffic jammed streets we could have a building-to-building system. This system could be built on one or more floor-to-floor levels and that includes the upper floors of adjourning skyscrapers.

(Public Domain picture of A South view of Kazi Nazrul Islam Ave Road from Paribag foot over bridge, Dhaka.)

This in turn can eliminate many parking garages and on street parking in that high speed people movers could bring citizens from long distances out of the city to the city and junction stations. In effect, a high speed subway or covered walkway that is built in the sky instead of underground.

By eliminating street traffic we can cut the cost of police and parking enforcements, street maintenance including trash and snow removal, traffic control markings, signs, and lights; and the highly polluted and dangerous air caused by vehicles of all types.

"High-speed rail clearly offers a path to lower greenhouse gas emissions than other modes of transportation. If HSR services can entice people out of their cars by offering convenience and speed at a low cost, this would significantly reduce societal energy consumption and carbon emissions. The California High-Speed Rail Authority (CHSRA), for example, estimates that by 2040, California's HSR system will reduce vehicle miles of travel in the state by 10 million miles each day; over a 58-year period, the system will reduce auto traffic on the state's highways by over 400 billion miles of travel. In addition, CHSRA estimates that starting in 2030, the state will see a reduction of 93 to 171 flights daily, which translates into improved air quality and improved health, along with the economic benefits of a more energy-efficient transportation system."

REF: https://www.eesi.org/papers/view/fact-sheet-high-speed-rail-development-worldwide

As a note of interest, some cities like London and New York City are starting to implement 'Congestion Taxes'. These are fees for entering the city by a vehicle that is other than public transportation, walking, biking, or motorcycling.

Section # 10 – Freight Movers:

We currently move freight from an airport, seaport, farm, or factory by boat, airliner, truck, or railroad. The boats or ships can move many containers of 'stuff' from one port to another, usually from a foreign port to another foreign post. It is then unloaded unto trucks or train cars for transport to another destination that is usually a distribution warehouse from which it is further unloaded, sorted, and loaded on a train or truck to another destination.

(Public Domain picture of the inside of a freight storage warehouse - pallet racks in a food stock warehouse by Jandrinov)

Some materials may go through days if not weeks of travel from the point of initial packaging to the final destination. This is a situation that has a cause and effect of material damage, missing materials, stolen materials, rotted perishable goods, and items either not getting delivered or delivered to the wrong locations. In short, a very costly means of distribution.

Let's look at a HSR alternative. Use individual freight cars or container flatbeds that are self-propelled by electricity and computer controlled to arrive at a pickup location, wait to be loaded, and then routed directly to the destination. This will allow an item or container lot to be moved from say Los Angeles to New York City in less than twelve hours (@ 280 MPH) as opposed to two or more days by other means.

Moving at these speeds the chances of breakage, theft, and loss is vastly reduced and thus a major savings to the shippers, receivers, and the customers or clients. This also helps companies and offices that have Just in Time (JIT) practices for their business models.

> *"Many other factors, however, need to be considered when calculating the true financial costs of cargo loss, including supply interruption, higher insurance claim costs, expedited freight costs, lost revenues from canceled deliveries, and more."*

> *"In addition, the supply chain managers' companies are not the only ones affected by cargo loss. The National Cargo Security Council (NCSC) estimates that the global financial impact of cargo loss exceeds $50 billion annually. That is a high price to pass on to your customers."*

REF: https://www.inboundlogistics.com/articles/the-full-cost-of-cargo-losses/

Slow moving trucks and trains are one area of concern for law enforcement and corporate businesses as each is a prime target for having products hijacked. Today's freight trains may have as many as a hundred containers in tow, and at a reasonable estimate of $50,000 per container, that represents $5,000,000 to be insured. And yes, if even one is boarded and ripped off, there has to be police investigations, insurance payouts, and much more.

90% of all truck hijackings involve criminals who have inside knowledge

Business Insider SA Justin Brown,

> *Cargo theft interrupts the flow of goods in your supply chain and your ability to deliver product. Cargo crime has more hidden consequences to your bottom line than you might realize. It is not just the loss of the cargo you need to account for, but also the cost of supply chain interruptions, extra customer contact and service, criminal investigations, expedited deliveries for replacement shipments, rising insurance rates and even lost business.*

REF: https://www.inboundlogistics.com/articles/the-full-cost-of-cargo-losses/

(Picture from High altitude https://www.businessinsider.co.za/truck-hijackings-violence-criminals-heists-2020-2)

By using dedicated HSR Freight Mover container cars that do NOT need to stop and be unloaded many times, and can be routed from point 'a' to 'b' without stopping, we can cut cost of goods and wasted perishables greatly.

As a note of interest, there have been over 1,000 reported train derailments in the US in 2022, and these are due to aging and outdated tracks and rolling stock. As the current system continues to age there will be many more derailments and accidents and each is a hazard to the population that resides near the tracks; and each is a financial loss to those that operate or use the current passenger and freight train systems.

The newly proposed rail systems of HSR, MagLev, and Hyperloops have built in technology that tends to prevent derailments and thus, will be much safer as well as less expensive in the overall theme of things.

(Public Domain picture - Train wreck at Montparnasse Station, at Place de Rennes side (now Place du 18 Juin 1940), Paris, France, 1895.)

Section # 11 – The Future of HSR in the Americas:

The Americas, which include Alaska/USA, Canada, Mexico, Central America, and South America nearly goes from Pole to Pole and there are well over a billion people living and working, playing, and vacationing along the way.

We can and should build a HSR system for people, parcels, and food from the tip of Alaska to the tip of Argentina, and then spur it to every city we can. This will open up trillions of dollars in trade and provide jobs for tens of millions as track is laid, stations built, rolling stock constructed, power plants constructed, and new cities and businesses spring up along the routes. We in the USA can be, should be, MUST BE, the leader in this joint venture and we can profit greatly by supplying much of the engineering, materials, rolling stock, and labor for this.

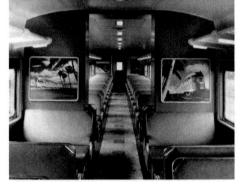

We once had The Budd Company that made fine passenger cars for the railroads, we need to recreate The Budd Company and be the number one supplier in the Western Hemisphere.

REF: https://hiddencityphila.org/2018/08/budd-company-an-industrial-icon-that-broke-the-mold/

(Public Domain picture by Lewis and Gilman, public relations for the Budd Company)

We can also export to Australia, India, and Africa, which are developing nations that will need our expertise and products. Remember that the low cost and freely available dirty coal and oil is NOT readily available in many nations, and they will need transportation that can run on renewables, which HSR can easily do. And these countries have an abundance of sunlight for powering their rail systems and thus, we open up their country with HSR, we open it to self-supporting businesses and such. China is already there, and it is bidding for the rights, we need to get our heads out of the sand and do the same; only better and cheaper.

TRAIN ©

The (Train) Rail Access Interstate Network (TRAIN) would be used to tie interstate tourism and commerce together throughout the USA. And the best part is that we already have much of it done in the form of US-35.  US-35 from Mexico to Canada and the Great Lakes is the backbone of the proposed transport system, with US -10, US-20, US-30, US-40, US-70, US-80, US-90, and US-94 being the ribs.

The roads are already in place, therefore the land and right-of-way are already paid for, thus it would be relatively inexpensive to add pipelines, solar panels, wind turbines, and high-speed rail transport along the length of each, paid for by TRIPS (Transportation and Regional Infrastructure Project Bonds), and other non-taxpayer funding.

(Public Domain picture Eastbound Interstate 78/U.S. Route 22 at mile marker 24.5 in Berks County, Pennsylvania.)

There is one such line in motion, it will be going from Tucson to Phoenix, Arizona and the 110 MPH semi-high-speed train will cut hours off of driving and flying times. What a **TRIP** !

(2023 update. The last administration failed to finance this HSR system)

Driving vs. Rail:
Where are you traveling? Is it one-way or round trip? What days of the week? Do you need to count meals and motels, gasoline differences from place to place, insurance, driver fatigue, etc.?

Amtrak.com has all sorts of methods of getting from one place to another, and it has comfortable seating and beds, as well as fine food service.. It also gives discounts to Seniors, AAA members, Veterans, etc., and if you play with their scheduling, day by day and week by week you can or will find many deals, or higher or lower prices for the same trips. (Supply and demand for seats).

And if you are taking the kids, they will get to sit in the Observation Cars, see the USA (Not in your Chevrolet). Amtrak also works with many touring agencies for package deals and car rentals, not always the lowest cost, but sometimes the best deal.

I also find that it sometimes pays to fly one-way, and take the train the other on the longer trips, it provides the best value for the buck.

Alaska to the tip of South America ©

If you draw a line on the world map from Alaska to the tip of South America you will see that it cuts through some of the wealthiest and the poorest economic areas in the world; you will also see that it cuts through some of the most abundant and least abundant areas of natural resources, water, minerals, etc.

Additionally, you will see that it cuts through many countries that have diverse cultures, ideals, and political aspirations.

(Picture is from the BorderTransportationSystem.com site)

What you do not see, but should, is the potential of this line. There are along this line a means of bringing vast wealth to hundreds of millions of people and companies; but there is one thing missing from the equation that can create this wealth that would come from opening areas of trade, tourism, proper use of natural resources, and a tremendous exchange of labor, both manual and mental.

(Update, in many of the South American Nations the High Speed Rail and People Movers are being built, but the US is not doing the building)

What is missing, a common means of transport that can carry material and people to and from the areas along the line that needs each. We have the Panama Canal; the Chinese are building a new Atlantic to Pacific Canal, both of which everyone claims is needed for passage and transport, but we do not have a land based Alaska to the tip of South America transportation passage means. We also do not have an Atlantic to Pacific high-speed transport system that can be used in the event of war or just for moving goods from one ocean to the other.

Consider building a High-Speed Rail system with corresponding roads, pipelines, and energy producing means that moves people and goods from Alaska to the tip of South America.

This would help end our illegal immigration problems, as there would be work for millions of people north and south of our borders as they build this, and as towns, factories, and tourism developed along its length.

(Picture of workers on the California HSR is from https://www.naco.org/articles/high-speed-rail-delivers-jobs-counties)

This project would provide means for millions to get out of impoverished areas, and can be the 'Backbone' of a network of 'Ribs' of similar transportation projects, which can keep developing for not just decades, but centuries. And the great part about this is that it can be self-supporting, self-sustaining, and done at little to no cost to the taxpayers, while generating tax revenue for other infrastructure projects, educational opportunities, and research for future projects.

Some will say that we have airlines for this purpose, but one has to look at the facts; airlines cannot carry the loads that railcars can, airlines need fossil fuels that surface transport does not, airline cost per pound per mile is going up, whereas surface transportation cost per pound per mile using clean wind and solar energy is going down.

Some will say that we have ocean going shipping for this purpose, and that is true, but you cannot build factories, towns, etc, along a route that a ship or aircraft transverses, you can build along roads and rails.

Let's do this; let's get our governments to put their collective heads together to create this basic transportation system that will finally unite the AMERICAS.

Section # 12 – Other Transport Mechanisms:

I would love to say that we will have the Star Trek Transporter by the year 2030, but I doubt that we will. What we may have is a village or city that has all the commercial buildings hooked to a miniature Hyperloop system that is hooked to all the residential buildings. This will allow items such as fast food or shopping center items to be 'transported' in minutes from the time of an

order to the consumer. One can be sure that Amazon or Walmart is already working on how to do this, as is McDonalds and Burger King.

If such a system is developed and used then the UPS, FedEx, and USPS could save billions in shipping costs, as they would not need any local delivery trucks and the associated cost of each, with driver.

When a new housing development is designed and approved, it would be the time to add the piping along with the pipes for gas, electric, and water.

(Picture is a Ford Motor Company delivery robot - https://corporate.ford.com/articles/products/autonomous-vehicle-robot-delivery.html)

Note that companies and shipping lines are looking into and are starting to build and implement autonomous robots and hovercrafts for doing both in house and outside deliveries.

In many cities around the world there are Micromobility devices that can be used on streets in residential and commercial neighborhoods. In Portugal the citizens have access to e-bikes and e-scooters on nearly every block in the shopping areas. Some have a fee associated, but most did not. You just get on and ride and then get off and leave the device for the next person's use.

In some cities they are experimenting with e-Vertical Takeoff and Landing cars and taxies that can fly over the traffic from location to location, thus saving time for those using the service.

(Picture of an e-VTOL Flying Car or Taxi https://www.diplomaticourier.com/posts/the-future-of-transportation-cars-trains-and-planes)

Space age jets that are more like a rocket or spacecraft may soon be able to fly above the earth at several thousand miles per hour. These may shorten a 7-hour trip from NYC to Lisbon to an hour or less. They will in effect be flying at about 60,000 feet above the ground and faster than sound.

Flying Hotel Pods are in the future. These will allow the 'hotel room' to be flown under its power to anywhere the clients desire, including the wilderness or to someone's back yard.

In short, we are at the tip of the iceberg when it comes to new and futuristic transportation and energy solutions. In the next two to three decades we will have major advances in Green Energy production, and in how we move people and stuff from point 'a' to 'b'.

We will be traveling to the moon and into outer space, and we will have floating cities here on earth and in the space between here in the moon. We will be controlled by Artificial Intelligence and it will keep us safe and secure in our travels.

There are only two things that can keep all of this from happening, and those are the greed of some, and the lack of vision by many.

Appendix I – Section Index

Appendix II – Reference Links

This section contains dozens of Internet website page addresses that you may find interesting. Three dots (…) means that from this page you can access several other associated topic pages. All the following links were tested as valid on February 18, 2023.

Biogas Information …
https://energypedia.info/wiki/Electricity_Generation_from_Biogas

Biofuel Basics
https://www.energy.gov/eere/bioenergy/biofuel-basics

Border Transportation System …
http://www.bordertransportationsystem.com

Energy and Fuels
https://www.iea.org/fuels-and-technologies

Federal Railroad Administration …
https://dotcms.fra.dot.gov/federal-state-partnership-intercity-passenger

High Speed Rail Data – (As of 2011) …
https://www.highspeed-rail.org/Pages/BasicFacts.aspx

High Speed Rail Information …
https://search.usa.gov/search?affiliate=fra&query=downloads%20for%20intercity%20high%20speed%20rail%20plan&commit=Search

Hyperloop – How it works
https://tumhyperloop.com/about-hyperloop/

MagLev – How it works
https://www.energy.gov/articles/how-maglev-works

National Rail Plan for the US

https://dotcms.fra.dot.gov/sites/fra.dot.gov/files/fra_net/1336/NRP_Sept2010_WEB.pdf

Northeast Corridor Funding & Improvements
https://dotcms.fra.dot.gov/about-fra/communications/newsroom/press-releases/biden-harris-administration-usdot-make-available-1

Passenger High Speed Rail Projects …
https://uic.org/passenger/highspeed/

Personal Rapid Transit – How it Works
https://www.railway-technology.com/projects/personal-rapid-transit/

Pneumatic Tubes – How it Works …
https://pneumatic.tube/how-it-works

Routing Maps of HSR around the world
https://www.eesi.org/papers/view/fact-sheet-high-speed-rail-development-worldwide

Tilting Trains – How it Works
https://www.railway-technology.com/projects/pendolino-train/

Transportation Updates …
https://dailyupdate.transportation.org/Pages/DailyUpdate.aspx

Underwater Bullet Trains – How it Works (With Reader Comments)
https://thedailychina.org/china-is-building-its-first-underwater-bullet-train/

Vactrain – How it Works (Very Long PDF)
https://web.wpi.edu/Pubs/E-project/Available/E-project-101207-130034/unrestricted/IQP.pdf

Appendix III – Abbreviations

These are used throughout the book.

AI	Artificial Intelligence
ATC	Air Traffic Control
ATS	Airport Transit System
AC	Alternating Current
AGT	Automated Guideway Transit
APM	Automated People Movers
ATN	Automated Transit Networks
AAVs	Autonomous Aerial Vehicles
BART	Bay Area Rapid Transport
BBC	British Broadcasting Company
B2B	Business to Business
CBP	Immigration Customs and Border Protection
CO2	Carbon Dioxide
CEC	Climate Energy Contribution
CDL	Commercial Driver's License
DoD	Department of Defense
DOT	Department of Transportation
DPM	Detroit People Mover
DTC	Detroit Transportation Corporation
DC	Direct Current
EV	Electric Vehicle
EPA	Environment Protection Agency
FTA	Federal Transit Administration
FMHSRS	Freight Mover High Speed Rail
GPS	Global Positioning System
HSR	High-Speed Rail
HOA	Homeowner Associations
H	Hydrogen
H2O	Water
JIT	Just in Time
LMOP	Landfill Methane Outreach Program
LRT	Light Rail Transit
MAAS	Mobility as a Service
MPH	Miles per Hour
MMF	Multi-Modal Facility
NPS	National Park Service
NTSB	National Transportation Safety Board
O	Oxygen
PRT	Personal Rapid Transit
RTA	Road Traffic Act
VTOL	Vertical Take-Off and Landing

Index:

107

Author:

The author has worked as an engineering technician, engineering designer, and inventor with experts in the transportation, touring, engineering, construction, manufacturing, IC, nuclear, oceanographic, missile, technical writing, pharmaceutical, and communications industries. He has over 50 years of experience that include countless hours of research and development, as well as educational instruction, learned and taught.

Cover Picture:

Public Domain picture of A South view of Kazi Nazrul Islam Ave Road from Paribag foot over bridge, Dhaka.

See page 82.

"Dhaka was the capital of a proto-industrialised Mughal Bengal for 75 years (1608–39 and 1660–1704). It was the hub of the muslin trade in Bengal and is one of the most prosperous cities in South Asia" REF: Wikipedia

I chose this picture for the cover as it represents the future of transportation in the world, **IF** we do nothing to stop the current growth of people, roads, vehicles, and the associated use of fossil fuels and its pollution.

Going forward we can stop this from happening, and live better lives with faster transportation, cleaner air and water, and far less cost.

This is where we should be heading in all nations, all towns and cities for the next hundred years or more.

(Picture from https://www.diplomaticourier.com/posts/the-future-of-transportation-cars-trains-and-planes)

Printed in Great Britain
by Amazon

37033097R00066